VIRGINIA TEST PREP
Reading Skills Workbook
Focus on Fiction
Grade 5

© 2019 by V. Hawas

All rights reserved. No part of this book may be reproduced or transmitted in any form or by any means, electronic, mechanical, photocopying, recording, or otherwise without prior written permission.

ISBN 978-1689894944

TEST MASTER PRESS

www.testmasterpress.com

Reading Skills Workbook, Focus on Fiction, Grade 5

CONTENTS

Introduction   4

Reading Skills Practice Sets   5

Practice Set 1: Personal Narrative   5
Practice Set 2: Myth   14
Practice Set 3: Play   23
Practice Set 4: Historical Fiction   33
Practice Set 5: Fables   42
Practice Set 6: Science Fiction   53
Practice Set 7: Poetry   63
Practice Set 8: Nature Myths   74
Practice Set 9: Adventure Story   87
Practice Set 10: Mystery Story   96
Practice Set 11: Legend   106
Practice Set 12: Personal Narrative   116
Practice Set 13: Play   126
Practice Set 14: Poetry   136
Practice Set 15: Fairy Tale   147
Practice Set 16: Historical Fiction   157

Answer Key   169

INTRODUCTION
For Parents, Teachers, and Tutors

Virginia's English Language Arts Standards

Student learning and assessment in Virginia is based on the skills listed in the *Standards of Learning* and the *Curriculum Framework*. The reading standards describe how students will be able to read and comprehend fictional texts, literary nonfiction, and poetry. This workbook focuses specifically on giving students experience with a wide range of fictional texts. It provides practice understanding, analyzing, and responding to texts and will develop all the skills that students need.

Understanding and Analyzing Fictional Texts

The state standards and the state tests both focus on using a broad range of challenging fictional texts. This workbook provides practice with a wide variety of passage types. It includes common passage types like myths, fables, personal narratives, and poetry. It also includes more unique types like plays, legends, and historical fiction.

For all the passage types, students are expected to demonstrate in-depth understanding. Students need to use close reading to analyze texts carefully and to look at texts critically. Students need to understand what a text says, as well as recognize craft and structure. Students also need to evaluate texts, respond to texts, and make connections between texts. At the same time, there is a strong focus on using evidence to support answers. This workbook focuses on developing the advanced skills that students are expected to have, while giving students experience with a wide variety of passage types.

Types of Reading Comprehension Questions

The state tests require students to read fictional passages and answer questions to show understanding of the text. The tests include a wide variety of questions, including technology-enhanced questions that use online features. Students will answer multiple choice questions, multiple-select questions where more than one answer is selected, text selection questions where words or sentences are highlighted, written answer questions, and graphic response questions where students complete a table, diagram, or web. This workbook provides practice with a wide range of question types, and each passage also ends with an essay question.

Preparing for the SOL Reading Assessments

Students will be assessed each year by taking the SOL Reading assessments. This workbook will help students master these assessments. It will ensure that students have the ability to analyze and respond to all types of fictional texts, while having the strong skills needed to excel on the test.

Practice Set 1

Personal Narrative

My Rotten Day at the Beach

Instructions

This set has one passage for you to read. The passage is followed by questions.

Read each question carefully. For each multiple choice question, fill in the circle for the correct answer. For other types of questions, follow the instructions given. Some of the questions require a written answer. Write your answer on the lines provided.

My Rotten Day at the Beach
By Elle Jenson

While everyone else in the class went on cruises or went to amusement parks during their spring breaks, I stayed home. My parents had to work every single day while I stayed home with the babysitter.

Finally, on the last Saturday of spring break, my dad managed to get the day off. Luckily, my mom was already home for the weekend. I thought we might do something awesome like go to Six Flags, but, no. They just wanted to go to the beach.

I know my parents wanted to do something fun that they thought I would like. Have they met me? I hate salt water because it burns my eyes and you get sand stuck in your hair for days. Seagulls squawk constantly and the sound drives me crazy! Still, I was determined to have a good time on the only day I didn't have to stay home.

There were a few things I did like about the beach. First, I like the ice cream at Ziggy's. He does the tallest spiral of ice cream you will ever see and still puts sprinkles on top. Second, I like looking for sea glass along the beach, especially under the pier where it piles up the most. Finally, I like that my parents let me drink grape soda. It is the only time they let me drink soda at all.

I should have probably said, even though I like these things about the beach, it was still a rotten day at the beach. But I did not know it was going to be rotten until we got there.

Imagine your perfect day at the beach. I would bet you are imagining that the water is not too cold, the sun is not too hot, and that the playground is open. While I did not say that I liked the playground, it was still something to do at the beach other than swim and play in the sand.

Well, we got to the beach and it was completely cloudy. Somehow, it was still incredibly hot! I had a sunburn before I could put on my sunscreen. Then, the water was completely cold. It was not just chilly. It was as cold as ice. I thought the playground would be great, but it was closed while they updated and repaired some of the equipment. Just my luck!

I decided to have a grape soda since everything else was not going well. I opened the cooler and found out that the grape sodas had all exploded. The cooler was filled with a sea of soda that nobody could drink. I sighed and closed the lid. I shook my head and wondered if anything would go right today.

I was still a bit upset about the grape soda. But if anything was going to cheer me up, it was going to be a tall Ziggy's ice cream cone. I guess most of the other kids were having the same rotten day as me, since the line nearly wrapped around the building. When I finally got to the front of the line, I ordered my favorite, a tall chocolate cone with chocolate sprinkles in a chocolate waffle cone. Yum, yum, yum!

The ice cream server grabbed a chocolate waffle cone and pulled the lever for the ice cream. No ice cream came out. The machine started making gurgling sounds and then melted ice cream started pouring from every faucet. This day could not get any worse.

I told my parents about what happened, so they promised to take me to the Ziggy's in downtown the next day. That ended up being pretty awesome because we also went to the aquarium and got chili cheese fries in the food court. But my day at the beach was still pretty rotten.

Finally, for my last attempt at making our trip to the beach something to remember, I walked over to the pier to collect some sea glass. I found a green piece and a white piece before stepping on something sharp. I looked down and saw blood on my big toe and a fishing hook sticking out!

I called for my dad. He came running over right away. As soon as he saw the blood, he carried me all the way to the car! Then we had to go to the doctor to get the hook out.

The next day, my parents took me downtown and showered me with yummy food, fun activities, and tasty grape soda. Even though my day at the beach was really rotten, the next day made up for it. I will never ever forget my rotten day at the beach!

This is what you might imagine a beautiful day at the beach is like. This is not how my day turned out!

1. Read this sentence from the passage.

   While everyone else in the class went on cruises or went to amusement parks during their spring breaks, I stayed home.

   How does Elle most likely feel about this?
   - Ⓐ guilty
   - Ⓑ jealous
   - Ⓒ proud
   - Ⓓ relieved

2. Based on the details in paragraphs 3 and 4, list **two** more things that Elle likes and dislikes about the beach.

   ### How Elle Feels About the Beach

Likes	Dislikes
the ice cream at Ziggy's	salt water burning her eyes

3. In paragraph 4, Elle refers to "the tallest spiral of ice cream you will ever see." Which literary technique is used in this statement?
   - Ⓐ exaggeration
   - Ⓑ metaphor
   - Ⓒ personification
   - Ⓓ symbolism

4 Select the sentence in paragraph 7 that uses a simile. Select the **one** correct answer.

☐ Well, we got to the beach and it was completely cloudy.

☐ Somehow, it was still incredibly hot!

☐ I had a sunburn before I could put on my sunscreen.

☐ Then, the water was completely cold.

☐ It was not just chilly.

☐ It was as cold as ice.

5 In paragraph 6, Elle describes what a perfect day at the beach is like. How is paragraph 7 related to this paragraph?

Ⓐ It explains the problems caused by this perfect day.

Ⓑ It shows that the day was just like this perfect day.

Ⓒ It tells how the day was different to this perfect day.

Ⓓ It describes what someone else thinks is a perfect day.

6 How does Elle most likely feel when she sees that the grape sodas have exploded?

Ⓐ amused

Ⓑ angry

Ⓒ disappointed

Ⓓ puzzled

7 According to the passage, what goes wrong with the ice cream?

- Ⓐ The store runs out.
- Ⓑ The machine breaks down.
- Ⓒ The line is too long.
- Ⓓ The ice cream melts in the heat.

8 Complete the diagram by describing the events that happen when Elle is looking for sea glass.

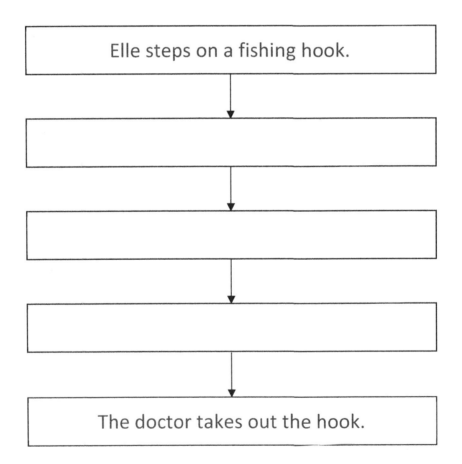

9 Read this sentence from the last paragraph.

> **The next day, my parents took me downtown and showered me with yummy food, fun activities, and tasty grape soda.**

What do these details suggest about the parents?

- Ⓐ They feel bad about how the day went.
- Ⓑ They wish they didn't have to work.
- Ⓒ They don't want Elle to get hurt.
- Ⓓ They want to go to the beach again.

10 Which of these can you mainly tell because the passage is written in first person point of view?

- Ⓐ where the events take place
- Ⓑ the order that things happened
- Ⓒ how Elle feels about the day
- Ⓓ why Elle spent the day at the beach

11 Why is Elle disappointed when her parents decide to go to the beach? Use **two** details from the passage to support your answer.

_____

_____

_____

_____

12 Elle describes how the line for ice cream "nearly wrapped around the building." Why would this make what happened when Elle ordered the ice cream worse? Explain.

_____

_____

_____

_____

13 After the problems with the ice cream, Elle says that the day "could not get any worse." Does the day actually get worse? Explain your answer.

_____

_____

_____

_____

14 According to the passage, why does Elle go under the pier?

    Ⓐ   to hide from everyone

    Ⓑ   to look for sea glass

    Ⓒ   to shelter from the sun

    Ⓓ   to go fishing

15 What do you think is the worst thing that goes wrong? Explain why you made that choice. Use details from the passage to support your answer.

Practice Set 2

Myth

The Lantern and the Fan

Instructions

This set has one passage for you to read. The passage is followed by questions.

Read each question carefully. For each multiple choice question, fill in the circle for the correct answer. For other types of questions, follow the instructions given. Some of the questions require a written answer. Write your answer on the lines provided.

The Lantern and the Fan

In a Japanese village there once lived a man who had two sons. When the sons were grown up, each brought home a wife from another village a long distance away. The father was greatly pleased with his two daughters-in-law. For many months, they all lived very happily together.

At last the two young wives asked to go home to visit their friends. Among the Japanese the sons and the sons' wives must always obey the father, so the two wives said, "Father-in-law, it is a long, long time since we have seen our friends. May we go to our old home and visit them?" The father-in-law answered, "No."

After many months they asked again, and again he answered, "No." Once more they asked. The father-in-law thought, "They care nothing for me, or they would not wish to leave me, but I have a plan, and I can soon know whether they love their father-in-law or not." Then he said to the older of the two wives, "You may go if you wish, but you must never come back unless you bring me fire wrapped in paper." To the younger he said, "You may go if you wish, but you must never come back unless you bring me wind wrapped in paper." The father-in-law thought, "Now I shall find out. If they care for me, they will search the country through till they find paper that will hold fire and wind."

The two young wives were so glad to visit their old friends that for almost a month they forgot all about the gifts that they were to carry to their father-in-law. At last, when it was time to go home, they were greatly troubled about what they must carry with them. They asked a wise man where to find the strange things. "Paper that will hold fire and wind!" he cried. "There is no such paper in Japan." The two women asked one wise man after another, and every one declared, "There is no such paper in Japan." What should they do? They feared they would never see their home again. They were so sad that they left their friends and wandered a long distance into the forest. Great tears fell from their eyes.

"I do not let people cry in my woods," said a voice. "My trees do not grow well in salt water."

The poor wives were so sorrowful that they forgot to be afraid, and the older one said, "Can we help crying? Unless I can carry to my father-in-law fire wrapped in paper, I can never go home." "And I," wailed the younger, "unless I can carry wind wrapped in paper, I can never go home. None of the wise men ever heard of such things. What shall we do?"

"It is easy enough to wrap fire in paper," answered the voice. "Here is a piece of paper. Now watch." They watched, and the strangest thing in all the world happened right before their eyes. There was no one to be seen, but a piece of paper appeared on the ground and folded itself into a Japanese lantern. "Now put a candle inside," said the voice, "and you have paper holding fire. What more could you ask?"

Then the older woman was happy, but the younger was still sad. She saw now that fire could be carried in paper, but surely no one could carry wind. "O dear voice," she cried, "can anyone carry wind in paper?"

"That is much easier than to carry fire," replied the voice, "for wind does not burn holes. Watch."

They watched eagerly. Another piece of paper came all by itself and lay on the ground between them. There was a picture on it of a tree covered with white blossoms. Two women stood under the tree, gathering the blossoms.

"The two women are yourselves," said the voice, "and the blossoms are the gifts that the father-in-law will give you when you go home."

"But I cannot go home," the younger wailed, "for I cannot carry wind wrapped in paper."

"Here is the paper, and there is always plenty of wind. Why not take them?"

"Indeed, I do not know how," the younger woman answered sorrowfully.

"This way, of course," said the voice. Some long, light twigs flew to the paper. It folded itself, over, under, together. It opened and closed, and it waved itself before the tearful face of the younger woman. "Does not the wind come to your face?" asked the voice, "and is it not the fan that has brought it? The lantern carries fire wrapped in paper, and the fan carries wind wrapped in paper."

Then, indeed, the two young women were happy, and when they came to the home of their father-in-law, he was as glad as they. He gave them beautiful gifts of gold and silver, and he said, "No one ever had such marvels before as the lantern and the fan, but in my home there are two more precious things than these, and they are my two dear daughters."

1 Which sentence from the first paragraph best shows that the father-in-law accepts his daughters-in-law?

- Ⓐ *In a Japanese village there once lived a man who had two sons.*
- Ⓑ *When the sons were grown up, each brought home a wife from another village a long distance away.*
- Ⓒ *The father was greatly pleased with his two daughters-in-law.*
- Ⓓ *For many months, they all lived very happily together.*

2 Read these words spoken by the wives.

> "Father-in-law, it is a long, long time since we have seen our friends. May we go to our old home and visit them?"

The way the wives speak mainly highlights that they are —

- Ⓐ homesick and sad
- Ⓑ polite and respectful
- Ⓒ nervous and afraid
- Ⓓ rude and demanding

3 Which word best describes how the wives look in the photograph at the beginning of the passage?

- Ⓐ content
- Ⓑ determined
- Ⓒ gloomy
- Ⓓ sneaky

4 Read this sentence from the passage.

> **At last, when it was time to go home, they were greatly troubled about what they must carry with them.**

Which one word could replace "greatly troubled" and have the same meaning?

- Ⓐ distressed
- Ⓑ exhausted
- Ⓒ furious
- Ⓓ startled

5 Paragraph 4 describes how the wives "wandered a long distance into the forest." Select the **two** words that describe moving in about the same way as the word *wandered* describes.

- ☐ ambled
- ☐ bounded
- ☐ glided
- ☐ raced
- ☐ roamed
- ☐ rushed
- ☐ snuck
- ☐ skipped

6 What do the wives reveal to the voice in paragraph 6?

- Ⓐ how frightened they feel
- Ⓑ how far from home they are
- Ⓒ what their plan is
- Ⓓ what the main problem is

7 Read this sentence from the passage.

> **They watched, and the strangest thing in all the world happened right before their eyes.**

Which literary technique is used in this sentence?

- Ⓐ alliteration
- Ⓑ hyperbole
- Ⓒ metaphor
- Ⓓ simile

8 Which dialogue spoken by the voice foreshadows that everything is going to work out fine in the end?

- Ⓐ *"I do not let people cry in my woods," said a voice. "My trees do not grow well in salt water."*
- Ⓑ *"Now put a candle inside," said the voice, "and you have paper holding fire. What more could you ask?"*
- Ⓒ *"The two women are yourselves," said the voice, "and the blossoms are the gifts that the father-in-law will give you when you go home."*
- Ⓓ *"Here is the paper, and there is always plenty of wind. Why not take them?"*

9 In the last paragraph, why does the father-in-law most likely describe the wives as precious?

- Ⓐ He now knows that they love him.
- Ⓑ He believes they have performed magic.
- Ⓒ He feels sorry for having doubted them.
- Ⓓ He hopes they will bring him more treasures.

10 Which statement describes what the passage is mainly about?

- Ⓐ two women accepting their place
- Ⓑ two women inventing new things
- Ⓒ two women proving their love
- Ⓓ two women finding their home

11 Which rule or custom that was part of Japanese culture at the time is described in paragraph 2? Use details from the paragraph to support your answer.

_____

_____

_____

_____

_____

12 In paragraph 4, the wives ask wise men for help. How do the wise men make the wives feel helpless? Use **two** details from the passage to support your answer.

_____

_____

_____

_____

_____

13 Explain how the fan carries wind. Use **two** details from the passage in your answer.

_____

_____

_____

_____

_____

14 Quests are a common feature of some myths and folktales. How does the passage involve a quest? Explain your answer.

_____

_____

_____

_____

_____

15 How does the passage show the importance of loyalty and respect? Use **three** details from the passage to support your answer.

Practice Set 3

Play

Christopher Columbus

Instructions

This set has one passage for you to read. The passage is followed by questions.

Read each question carefully. For each multiple choice question, fill in the circle for the correct answer. For other types of questions, follow the instructions given. Some of the questions require a written answer. Write your answer on the lines provided.

Christopher Columbus

ACT I

INTRODUCTION:

Christopher Columbus was born in Genoa, Italy, more than four hundred and fifty years ago. Genoa was a rich town on the Mediterranean Sea. She had trading routes to India, China, and Japan.

© Naci Yavuz/Shutterstock.com

Columbus was fond of stories of the sea and liked the study of geography. He was anxious to go to sea and while a boy made his first voyage. When he grew up to be a man, he went to Lisbon, the capital of Portugal. The bold deeds of Henry of Portugal drew many sailors to this city.

Lisbon was full of learned men and sailors longing to go on long voyages. These sailors had tried to find a shorter way to India but without success.

Columbus thought this could be done by going directly west. He thought the world round although most people at that time thought it flat. After many trials, he laid his plans before the Court of the King of Spain.

The first act will be Columbus at the Court of Spain.

(*King and Queen on throne—courtiers around.*)

(*Columbus enters and bows before king and queen.*)

Queen: You have come to us to talk about a shorter way to India?

Columbus: Yes, your Majesty. According to this map and the proof I have gathered, I believe India to be directly west. I have gone on long voyages and have talked to many sailors about the signs of land to the westward. I believe the world to be round and if your Majesty could aid me I know I could find this shorter route.

Queen: We would be glad indeed to aid you, but at the present time Spain has little money. The war has taken so much.

Wise Man of Spain: Your Majesty, this man thinks the world round. That is foolish. If you use your eyes you can see it is flat. To sail westward in the hope of getting to India is impossible and ridiculous.

Second Wise Man: Your Majesty, I think this man right. He says the world is round and I think if we study carefully, we will find it is so. If it is possible we should give him a chance.

ACT II

INTRODUCTION:

Columbus received little encouragement and after several years of waiting, set out to try his fortune in France. He stopped at a convent to beg for some bread. The Prior became interested in his plan and went to the Court of Spain, and begged the Queen not to allow Columbus to go to France but to help him in his plans.

The next act will be Columbus talking to the Queen.

Queen: Columbus, I will pledge my jewels in order to raise the money for a fleet. I will fit out an expedition and make you Governor over the land you discover.

Columbus: Thank you, your Majesty. The lands discovered will be taken up in the name of the King of Spain.

Queen: Will you take a vow to use the riches you obtain to help Spain prosper?

Columbus: I will take that vow.

Queen: I wish you safe travels and a successful outcome.

(*Columbus takes vow*).

ACT III

INTRODUCTION:

The voyage across the ocean was a long and tiresome one. The sailors became discouraged and wanted to return to Spain. Columbus kept on and finally was rewarded. The next act will be the discovery of land.

Columbus (*talking to sailors*): I rejoice my friends that you have had the strength to venture on with us. So many cheering signs have encouraged us to persevere. The birds in the air, the unusual fishes in the sea, and the plants seldom met far from rocks where they grow. I deem it probable that we reach the land this very night. I call on you all to be watchful.

(*Columbus and Luis walk apart from the other sailors. Columbus a little in advance, stops, calls Luis.*)

Columbus: Luis! Look in that direction, do you see anything uncommon?

Luis: I see a light, Senor.

Columbus: My eyes do not deceive me.

Luis: What think you, Don Christopher?

Columbus: Call Rodrigo Sanchez to come hither.

(*Rodrigo Sanchez comes. All look for light*).

Columbus: This is land. We will behold it soon.

(*Sailors rush up onto the deck. They all gaze out to the west. They push and jostle as they try to get in front to see better. They all exclaim, "Land! Land!"*)

Columbus: See the land, Luis?

Luis: Yes.

Columbus: Behold the Indies! Praise be to God!

1. Based on the details in the first introduction, list **two** beliefs Columbus had that caused him to believe he would find a shorter route to India.

   1: _____

   _____

   2: _____

   _____

2. According to Act I, what caused Spain to have little money?

   Ⓐ   disease

   Ⓑ   war

   Ⓒ   bad trades

   Ⓓ   poor weather

3. Read this line from the play.

   Wise Man of Spain: Your Majesty, this man thinks the world round. That is foolish. If you use your eyes you can see it is flat. To sail westward in the hope of getting to India is impossible and ridiculous.

   What does the word *ridiculous* mean?

   Ⓐ   very silly

   Ⓑ   very wasteful

   Ⓒ   very expensive

   Ⓓ   very dangerous

4   In Act I, what do the two wise men disagree about?

  Ⓐ   whether Columbus can be trusted

  Ⓑ   whether the world is flat or round

  Ⓒ   whether it is important to reach India faster

  Ⓓ   whether money should be spent exploring

5   Which sentence spoken by the Queen shows that she makes a personal sacrifice to help Columbus?

  Ⓐ   *Columbus, I will pledge my jewels in order to raise the money for a fleet.*

  Ⓑ   *I will fit out an expedition and make you Governor over the land you discover.*

  Ⓒ   *Will you take a vow to use the riches you obtain to help Spain prosper?*

  Ⓓ   *I wish you safe travels and a successful outcome.*

6   The introduction to Act III mainly suggests that Columbus was –

  Ⓐ   determined

  Ⓑ   foolish

  Ⓒ   intelligent

  Ⓓ   strict

7 In Columbus's first words in Act III, he refers to the "cheering signs" that land is near. Complete the web below by listing the **three** signs he mentions that suggest that land is near.

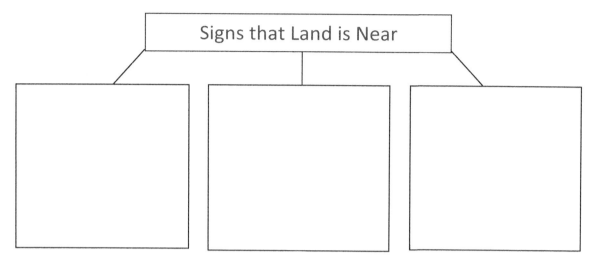

8 Read these lines from Act III of the play.

> **Columbus: Luis! Look in that direction, do you see anything uncommon?**
>
> **Luis: I see a light, Senor.**
>
> **Columbus: My eyes do not deceive me.**
>
> **Luis: What think you, Don Christopher?**

These lines mainly create a sense of –

Ⓐ   anger

Ⓑ   fear

Ⓒ   hope

Ⓓ   pride

9 Read this line from Act III of the play.

Columbus: Call Rodrigo Sanchez to come hither.

What does this line mean?

- Ⓐ Tell Rodrigo Sanchez to be quiet.
- Ⓑ Tell Rodrigo Sanchez to come here.
- Ⓒ Tell Rodrigo Sanchez to look around.
- Ⓓ Tell Rodrigo Sanchez to slow the ship.

10 Describe **two** details that help show the excitement the sailors feel when they see land.

1: _____

_____

2: _____

_____

11 According to the play, what was Columbus's main purpose for the journey?

- Ⓐ winning the Queen's approval
- Ⓑ proving that the Earth is round
- Ⓒ finding a shorter route to India
- Ⓓ claiming more land for Spain

12 In Act I, Columbus says that he believes that India is directly west. How can you tell that Columbus has done research on the topic? Explain your answer.

_____

_____

_____

_____

_____

13 In Act II, why does Columbus almost leave Spain? What causes him to stay in Spain? Use **two** details from the play to support your answer.

_____

_____

_____

_____

_____

14 How is Act II a success for Columbus? Explain your answer.

_____

_____

_____

_____

_____

15 How does the play show that Columbus has to overcome challenges to achieve success? Use **three** details from the play in your answer.

Practice Set 4

Historical Fiction

Working on the Railroad

Instructions

This set has one passage for you to read. The passage is followed by questions.

Read each question carefully. For each multiple choice question, fill in the circle for the correct answer. For other types of questions, follow the instructions given. Some of the questions require a written answer. Write your answer on the lines provided.

Working on the Railroad

In the year 1865 in California, three men had been working since dawn putting down a section of the transcontinental railroad. Transcontinental means crossing a continent, and these men were working for Central Pacific. Central Pacific were tasked with the job of laying down a railroad that would cross America. Central Pacific were starting the railroad in Sacramento, California, and building east until they connected with the railroad being built from the other company.

One of the men was Charlie Rubin. Charlie was an American who was born and raised in Sacramento, California. He was proud to be working on this mission, especially because of what it meant for travel. "One day," Charlie would say each day on the job, "when this railroad is built, I am taking my whole family across the country to see the Atlantic Ocean."

Charlie had a newborn baby at home and hoped to show his daughter the country when she grew older. His wife, Lillian, worried about Charlie every day. There were many dangers where he was working. Their job involved placing parts of the track above a deep canyon. The workers had to practice caution when laboring at such great heights. They also had to be sure to stay hydrated in the intense heat. Lillian made sure Charlie had two canteens, and Charlie made sure to finish both each day.

The two other men on this three-men team were brothers from China, Li and Jiang. Li and Jiang were Chinese immigrants who found work together, after a long search for a job, and were committed to being hard-working and successful to keep their employment. The brothers shared Charlie's dream of traveling across the United States. They had come to California during the Gold Rush and had stayed ever since.

Li was the older of the two brothers and was the primary caretaker of their aging parents. Every pay day, Li would send home all the money he could to his parents. The farther away they got, the more Li worried about his parents. He wondered how much longer he could work before he had to go home to tend to them.

Jiang was less concerned with responsibility. When he and his brother got the job on the railroad, he couldn't wait to get out of his small house. Ever since he and his family had emigrated from China, Jiang longed to see the United States. Money was tight, and he and Li had been searching for a job for months before they landed this assignment with Central Pacific. Jiang saw it as his opportunity for escape.

The three men had been working on this section of track for days and, although they kept to themselves at first, had become friendly over shared dreams to pass the long hours.

"Charlie," Li said as their first break drew closer, "if you were rich, what would be the first thing you'd buy?"

"Binoculars," Charlie said right away. Li and Jiang broke into laughter.

"Binoculars?" Jiang pressed. "Surely you can buy yourself a pair of binoculars. Why are they so important?"

"I would buy myself a pair of golden binoculars," Charlie explained. "I would sit on my porch in Sacramento and use my binoculars to see across the country. I'd wave to all the friends I will one day make on the east coast and admire the work of the railroad."

"Alright," Li replied, "fair enough." He continued nailing the rods into the ground.

"Know what I'd buy?" Jiang asked. Li and Charlie looked at him expectantly.

"I'd hire my personal stage coach in every state. I would hop from coach to coach until I reached the east coast, and I'd never look at another railway track again in my life."

Li and Charlie laughed in agreement.

"I'd buy a house for each of us," Li said with excitement. "We'd live on a beach in a neighborhood of our own. We wouldn't lift a finger. All we would do would be travel the world and then come back to our beach to relax."

All three men stopped working briefly to imagine this beautiful dream scenario. Then, it was time for a break. The men went back to their rickety tents and heated up leftover potatoes over a makeshift fire.

As the time passed, not one person spoke. Each man was lost in his own dream as he ate days-old potatoes and nursed his sore muscles. After work that day, each man would return to his tent and continue dreaming about a future of possibility. Laying down track by track, Charlie, Li, and Jiang envisioned each mile to be leading to that future, however impossible it may have seemed.

Reading Skills Workbook, Focus on Fiction, Grade 5

1	Use details from the passage to answer the questions below.

What year is the story set? _____

In what state is the story set? _____

What company do the characters work for? _____

What feature are they building? _____

2	What does the Latin prefix in the word *transcontinental* mean?
- Ⓐ	across
- Ⓑ	after
- Ⓒ	against
- Ⓓ	around

3	What would most help readers understand the path and distance of the completed railroad?
- Ⓐ	graph
- Ⓑ	map
- Ⓒ	photograph
- Ⓓ	timeline

4   Based on the information in paragraph 3, describe **two** reasons the work is dangerous.

1: _____

_____

2: _____

_____

5   Which detail given about Li and Jiang describes one way they are similar to Charlie?
- Ⓐ   They searched a long time before finding work.
- Ⓑ   They dream of traveling across the United States.
- Ⓒ   They previously worked in the gold fields of California.
- Ⓓ   They are immigrants seeking a better life for their families.

6   Based on the information in paragraph 5, which word best describes Li?
- Ⓐ   adventurous
- Ⓑ   cautious
- Ⓒ   determined
- Ⓓ   responsible

7 Read this sentence from the passage.

> **Money was tight, and he and Li had been searching for a job for months before they landed this assignment with Central Pacific.**

What does the phrase "money was tight" show?

- Ⓐ Jiang and Li kept losing their money.
- Ⓑ Jiang and Li saved most of their money.
- Ⓒ Jiang and Li did not have much money.
- Ⓓ Jiang and Li worked hard for their money.

8 The dream that Jiang describes involves hiring stage coaches in every state. What does this dream mainly reveal about him?

- Ⓐ He does not believe the railroad will be safe.
- Ⓑ He doubts the railroad will ever be finished.
- Ⓒ He is tired of looking at railroad tracks every day.
- Ⓓ He is proud of the part he is playing in making the railroad.

9 Which phrase best summarizes what the three men are doing as they talk?

- Ⓐ dreaming of the future
- Ⓑ complaining about their lives
- Ⓒ learning about each other's background
- Ⓓ developing a plan to escape their situation

10 Read these sentences spoken by Li.

> "We'd live on a beach in a neighborhood of our own. We wouldn't lift a finger. All we would do would be travel the world and then come back to our beach to relax."

What do Li's words suggest he dislikes most about his job?

- Ⓐ the loneliness
- Ⓑ the poor food
- Ⓒ the hard work
- Ⓓ the intense heat

11 The last two paragraphs reveal specific details about how difficult daily life is for the workers. List **three** details that show that their lives are difficult.

1: _____

2: _____

3: _____

12 Read this sentence from the last paragraph.

> Laying down track by track, Charlie, Li, and Jiang envisioned each mile to be leading to that future, however impossible it may have seemed.

What lesson is suggested by this sentence?

- Ⓐ Take it one day at a time.
- Ⓑ Appreciate what you have.
- Ⓒ There is no need to fear change.
- Ⓓ The best times are shared with friends.

13 How do you think the railroad being built would change travel for people living at the time? Use **two** details from the passage to support your answer.

_____

_____

_____

_____

_____

14 How do Charlie's binoculars represent the future he imagines? Use **two** details from the passage to support your answer.

_____

_____

_____

_____

_____

15 Charlie, Li, and Jiang have very different backgrounds, but their work on the railroad brings them together. Describe how their situation and shared dreams bring them together. Use **three** details from the passage to support your answer.

Practice Set 5

Fables

Set of Two Fables

Instructions

This set has two passages for you to read. Each passage is followed by questions.

Read each question carefully. For each multiple choice question, fill in the circle for the correct answer. For other types of questions, follow the instructions given. Some of the questions require a written answer. Write your answer on the lines provided.

The Town Mouse and the Country Mouse

A town mouse once visited a relative who lived in the country. For lunch the country mouse served wheat stalks, roots, and acorns, with a dash of cold water for drink. The town mouse ate very sparingly, nibbling a little of this and a little of that, and by her manner making it quite obvious that she ate the simple food only to be polite.

After the meal the friends had a long talk, or rather the town mouse talked about her life in the city while the country mouse listened. They then went to bed in a cozy nest in the hedgerow and slept in quiet and comfort until morning. In her sleep the country mouse dreamed she was a town mouse with all the luxuries and delights of city life that her friend had described for her. So the next day when the town mouse asked the country mouse to go home with her to the city, she gladly said yes.

When they reached the mansion in which the town mouse lived, they found on the table in the dining room the leavings of a very fine banquet. There were sweetmeats and jellies, pastries, delicious cheeses, indeed, the most tempting foods that a mouse can imagine.

But just as the country mouse was about to nibble a dainty bit of pastry, she heard a cat mew loudly and scratch at the door. In great fear the mice scurried to a hiding place, where they lay quite still for a long time, hardly daring to breathe. When at last they ventured back to the feast, the door opened suddenly and in came the servants to clear the table. When the servants had left, in came the house dog. It sniffed around every corner and the country mouse was sure she'd be found.

The country mouse stopped in the town mouse's den only long enough to pick up her carpet bag and umbrella.

"You may have luxuries and dainties that I have not," she said as she hurried away, "but I prefer my simple food and my simple life in the country with the peace and security that go with it."

1   Complete the web below by listing **four** items the country mouse served the town mouse.

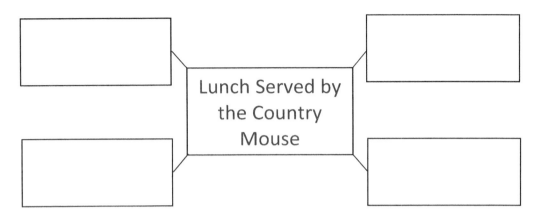

2   List **two** details the author includes to show that the town mouse did not eat much of the country mouse's lunch.

1: _____

_____

2: _____

_____

3   The town mouse would most likely describe the country mouse's food as —

Ⓐ   too old

Ⓑ   too fancy

Ⓒ   too plain

Ⓓ   too strange

4 Which sentence from paragraph 2 best shows that the country mouse's life is peaceful?

- Ⓐ *After the meal the friends had a long talk, or rather the town mouse talked about her life in the city while the country mouse listened.*
- Ⓑ *They then went to bed in a cozy nest in the hedgerow and slept in quiet and comfort until morning.*
- Ⓒ *In her sleep the country mouse dreamed she was a town mouse with all the luxuries and delights of city life that her friend had described for her.*
- Ⓓ *So the next day when the town mouse asked the country mouse to go home with her to the city, she gladly said yes.*

5 In paragraph 2, how does the town mouse talking about her life affect the country mouse?

- Ⓐ It makes the country mouse want to experience the city life.
- Ⓑ It makes the country mouse appreciate her own life.
- Ⓒ It makes the country mouse afraid of living in a city.
- Ⓓ It makes the country mouse feel embarrassed.

6 Describe **two** details from paragraph 2 that support your answer to Question 5.

1: _____

_____

2: _____

_____

7 How is the food at the town mouse's home different to what the country mouse served? Use **two** details from the passage to support your answer.

_____

_____

_____

_____

_____

8 Complete the diagram below by listing the three events that frightened the country mouse and stopped her from eating. List the events in order from first to last.

Events that Frightened the Country Mouse

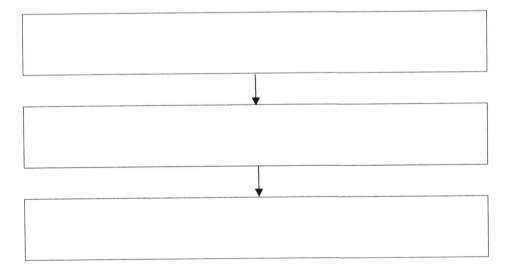

9 Why does the country mouse decide to leave and return home? In your answer, describe the lesson she learns while visiting the town mouse.

_____

_____

_____

_____

_____

10 At the end of the passage, what does the country mouse value most about her home?

- Ⓐ not having to travel far
- Ⓑ feeling safe there
- Ⓒ spending time alone
- Ⓓ eating the foods that she likes

The Rooster and the Fox

One bright evening as the sun was sinking on a glorious world a wise old rooster flew into a tree to roost. Before he composed himself to rest, he flapped his wings three times and crowed loudly. But just as he was about to put his head under his wing, his beady eyes caught a flash of red and a glimpse of a long pointed nose, and there just below him stood Master Fox.

"Have you heard the wonderful news?" cried the fox in a very joyful and excited manner.

"What news?" asked the rooster very calmly. But he had a strange, fluttery feeling inside him, for, you know, he was very much afraid of the fox.

"Your family and mine and all other animals have agreed to forget their differences and live in peace and friendship from now on forever. Just think of it! I simply cannot wait to embrace you! Do come down, dear friend, and let us celebrate the joyful event."

"How grand!" said the rooster. "I certainly am delighted at the news." But he spoke in an absent way, and stretching up on tiptoes, seemed to be looking at something far off.

"What is it you see?" asked the fox a little anxiously.

"Why, it looks to me like a couple of dogs coming this way. They must have heard the good news and—"

But the fox did not wait to hear more. Off he started on a run.

"Wait," cried the rooster. "Why do you run? The dogs are friends of yours now!"

"Yes," answered the fox. "But they might not have heard the news. Besides, I have a very important errand that I had almost forgotten about."

The rooster smiled as he buried his head in his feathers and went to sleep, for he had succeeded in outwitting a very crafty enemy.

Reading Skills Workbook, Focus on Fiction, Grade 5

1 Read this sentence from the passage.

> **One bright evening as the sun was sinking on a glorious world a wise old rooster flew into a tree to roost.**

What is the main purpose of this sentence?

- Ⓐ to describe the main problem
- Ⓑ to introduce the setting
- Ⓒ to highlight the theme
- Ⓓ to tell who the main characters are

2 In the first paragraph, what is the rooster about to do when the fox interrupts him?

- Ⓐ go to sleep
- Ⓑ have a meal
- Ⓒ sing a song
- Ⓓ fly away

3 Read these sentences that describe the rooster's response to the fox.

> **"What news?" asked the rooster very calmly. But he had a strange, fluttery feeling inside him, for, you know, he was very much afraid of the fox.**

This response mainly suggests that the rooster is being –

- Ⓐ cautious
- Ⓑ dishonest
- Ⓒ jealous
- Ⓓ rude

Reading Skills Workbook, Focus on Fiction, Grade 5

4 Describe **two** ways the fox tries to seem positive and enthusiastic in paragraph 4.

1: _____

_____

2: _____

_____

5 Read this statement made by the fox.

Besides, I have a very important errand that I had almost forgotten about.

What is the fox doing when he makes this statement?

- Ⓐ stating a fact
- Ⓑ making an excuse
- Ⓒ telling an opinion
- Ⓓ giving a compliment

6 In the last line, the fox is described as "a very crafty enemy." What does this tell the reader about the fox?

- Ⓐ He is sly and sneaky.
- Ⓑ He enjoys making things.
- Ⓒ He is uncaring and mean.
- Ⓓ He gets bored easily.

7   In paragraph 4, what is the fox trying to trick the rooster into doing? Use details from the passage to support your answer.

   _____
   _____
   _____
   _____
   _____

8   Does the rooster believe the fox's statement that all the animals have agreed to forget their differences and live in peace and friendship? Use details from the passage to support your answer.

   _____
   _____
   _____
   _____
   _____

Reading Skills Workbook, Focus on Fiction, Grade 5

9 How is saying that there are dogs coming a way to test the fox? Use details from the passage to support your answer.

_____

_____

_____

_____

_____

10 Circle the word below that best describes the rooster. Then explain how the passage shows that the rooster has this quality.

    clever   trusting   foolish   lazy

_____

_____

_____

_____

_____

Practice Set 6

Science Fiction

Mayor Renna's Letter

Instructions

This set has one passage for you to read. The passage is followed by questions.

Read each question carefully. For each multiple choice question, fill in the circle for the correct answer. For other types of questions, follow the instructions given. Some of the questions require a written answer. Write your answer on the lines provided.

Mayor Renna's Letter

The clock projection flashed to 11:42 p.m. on May 7, 2072. In only eighteen minutes, Linda Renna would become Mayor Renna. While she should have been happy about her victory, Linda was pacing back and forth in her office in a panic. She clenched and unclenched her fists, but still she just couldn't relax.

Linda had received the phone call hours ago announcing that she had won the race for mayor of her town, Gemville. Most winners would be celebrating, but Linda had a deadline to make. Linda needed to write an acceptance letter to her citizens by midnight. At that time, her Data Delivery Drone (D3 for short), would immediately issue the letter to every citizen of Gemville. With eighteen minutes remaining, Linda had nothing written. The deadline was coming up fast, and Linda didn't know what to do.

Linda stared at her mindtyper with fury. This device did not require a single key to be hit to compose a written document. All you had to do was look at the device and it would read your mind and your thoughts would appear on the screen. Usually, this was a great way to communicate quickly and easily. But on this night, Linda's anxious thoughts were getting in the way of writing what she really wanted to say.

The device whirred to life and typed Linda's current thoughts:

Dear Citizens of Gemville,

I can't do it. I am not prepared. Why did I enter this race for mayor in the first place? Did I really think I could make a difference? Gemville needs someone with confidence. I am not that person. I am truly terrified.

"Mindtyper, SWEEP," Linda spoke aloud, and the mindtyper cleared the screen. Linda walked away, fearful that her thoughts would again appear in front of her.

The clock projection grew on her wall with each minute that passed. Now, 11:49 p.m. covered almost the entire wall. "Eleven minutes to delivery," barked her D3. Linda shouted back, "I KNOW!"

As Linda turned back towards her mindtyper, she tried to clear her head and think the words she had rehearsed before. After getting out one line that stated she was grateful for the position, her mind would switch and the next line would reveal how worried and uncertain she felt. Her time was almost up. In only six minutes, her mindtyper would deliver her words to every citizen of Gemville.

A scratch on her door woke Linda up from her anxious trance. Linda snapped her fingers twice and her automated door lifted off the ground to allow her dog, Tut, into her office. Tut had sensed Linda's pain and bounded into Linda's arms. After giving her many kisses, Tut strutted over to the mindtyper, stood on his hind legs and stared into the screen. Linda pulled her chair back to her desk as the screen filled with Tut's thoughts.

Stop worrying about letting Gemville down, Tut's thoughts translated. *Remember why you ran for mayor. Remember when you were a little girl trying to get on the public transport bus and it was never on time? Remember when you were applying to college and the library had only two mindtypers to use? You waited hours only to be kicked off after 30 minutes of staring blankly at the screen! You can make changes here. You just have to believe in yourself and be honest with your citizens.*

Tut looked back at his master. He had the puppy dog eyes down to a science. How could Linda argue with this furry companion?

"You're right, Tut," Linda exclaimed. "I've got this! I won the race because I am capable, and I can make important changes in this town. It's time for me to start."

Tut barked in reply, then slipped under the door to give Linda her privacy. Linda cracked her knuckles and looked out the window to prepare herself. Linda swiped her fingers across her window to reveal different views of her town. She saw the park, the bus, the library, and finally the calm of the neighborhoods with her citizens fast asleep. Linda turned to her mindtyper with two minutes to spare and allowed her heart to spill onto the screen.

Dear Gemville,

Thank you for trusting me with the job of mayor. I entered this race because I believed a lot could be done for this town. As someone who has grown up in Gemville, I have seen the beauty it has to offer, but also the big strides it must take to become worthy of its great citizens. I promise to always keep your interests at heart. To be honest, this letter has taken me a long time to write. I am admittedly nervous because I want to be enough for Gemville and want to be the mayor you all need me to be. At the same time, I know that with the help of all of you we can polish this town into a true gem.

Thank you again, and please remember to reach out to me at any time with your concerns or suggestions.

Yours,

Mayor Renna

With the last punctuation typed, the clock struck midnight and Linda's D3 lit up and processed her letter. Tut came barreling back into her room and sat on Linda's lap.

You did it! I knew you could! Tut mindtyped.

Reading Skills Workbook, Focus on Fiction, Grade 5

1 What main problem is introduced in the first two paragraphs?

- Ⓐ Linda did not expect to become mayor.
- Ⓑ Linda has to write an acceptance letter.
- Ⓒ Linda does not know what being the mayor involves.
- Ⓓ Linda is having trouble getting her mindtyper to work.

2 Describe **two** of Linda's actions from the first paragraph that reveal that she is feeling anxious.

1: _____

_____

2: _____

_____

3 Read this sentence from the passage.

> **The deadline was coming up fast and Linda didn't know what to do.**

Which of these would be the best word to replace "coming up fast" to create a sense of dread?

- Ⓐ approaching
- Ⓑ looming
- Ⓒ nearing
- Ⓓ slinking

4 Which sentence from paragraph 3 reveals why Linda is unable to write her letter?

- Ⓐ *This device did not require a single key to be hit to compose a written document.*
- Ⓑ *All you had to do was look at the device and it would read your mind and your thoughts would appear on the screen.*
- Ⓒ *Usually, this was a great way to communicate quickly and easily.*
- Ⓓ *But on this night, Linda's anxious thoughts were getting in the way of writing what she really wanted to say.*

5 What does the first letter that Linda writes mainly help the reader understand?

- Ⓐ why Linda became mayor
- Ⓑ how much self-doubt Linda feels
- Ⓒ how Linda has to write the letter quickly
- Ⓓ why Linda cares so much about being mayor

6 Read these sentences from the passage.

> **The clock projection grew on her wall with each minute that passed. Now, 11:49 p.m. covered almost the entire wall. "Eleven minutes to delivery," barked her D3. Linda shouted back, "I KNOW!"**

Which word best describes the mood of these sentences?

- Ⓐ fearful
- Ⓑ gloomy
- Ⓒ mysterious
- Ⓓ tense

7 Read this sentence from the passage.

> **After getting out one line that stated she was grateful for the position, her mind would switch and the next line would reveal how worried and uncertain she felt.**

What does this sentence reveal about Linda?

- Ⓐ She is too tired to think clearly.
- Ⓑ She is not honestly happy to be mayor.
- Ⓒ Her excitement is confusing her mindtyper.
- Ⓓ Her negative thoughts keep getting in the way.

8 The mindtyper reveals Tut's thoughts to Linda. Based on Tut's thoughts, what does he want Linda to focus on?

- Ⓐ how educated she is
- Ⓑ what she has been through
- Ⓒ what she hopes to achieve
- Ⓓ how much the citizens adore her

9 Right before she writes the second letter, the author describes how Linda "allowed her heart to spill onto the screen." This phrase mainly suggests that the letter is –

- Ⓐ sad and emotional
- Ⓑ honest and sincere
- Ⓒ positive and uplifting
- Ⓓ somber and serious

10 Underline **three** phrases from the letter that Linda writes that reveal that she wants to make changes and improve Gemville.

Thank you for trusting me with the job of mayor. I entered this race because I believed a lot could be done for this town. As someone who has grown up in Gemville, I have seen the beauty it has to offer, but also the big strides it must take to become worthy of its great citizens. I promise to always keep your interests at heart. To be honest, this letter has taken me a long time to write. I am admittedly nervous because I want to be enough for Gemville and want to be the mayor you all need me to be. At the same time, I know that with the help of all of you we can polish this town into a true gem.

11 The author begins the passage by stating the exact time. How does the time help explain Linda's feelings at the start of the passage? Use **two** details from the passage to support your answer.

_____

_____

_____

_____

12 According to the passage, a mindtyper reads minds and puts thoughts on the screen. Why is this device important in allowing Tut to help Linda? Explain your answer.

_____

_____

_____

_____

_____

13 How does the final letter that Linda writes show that she cares about Gemville? Use **two** details from the letter to support your answer.

_____

_____

_____

_____

_____

14 Which phrase best summarizes the main lesson that Linda learns?

Ⓐ   Stay humble.

Ⓑ   Believe in yourself.

Ⓒ   Don't be afraid of change.

Ⓓ   Preparation is the key to success.

15. The turning point of the passage occurs when Tut's thoughts are revealed to Linda. Explain how reading Tut's thoughts changes how Linda feels. Use **three** details from the passage in your answer.

Practice Set 7

Poetry

Set of Two Poems

Instructions

This set has two passages for you to read. Each passage is followed by questions.

Read each question carefully. For each multiple choice question, fill in the circle for the correct answer. For other types of questions, follow the instructions given. Some of the questions require a written answer. Write your answer on the lines provided.

Little by Little

"Little by little," an acorn said,
As it slowly sank in its mossy bed,
"I am improving every day,
Hidden deep in the earth away."
Little by little, each day it grew;
Little by little, it sipped the dew;

Downward it sent out a thread-like root;
Up in the air sprung a tiny shoot.
Day after day, and year after year,
Little by little the leaves appear;
And the slender branches spread far and wide,
Till the mighty oak is the forest's pride.

"Little by little," said a thoughtful boy,
"Moment by moment, I'll well employ,
Learning a little every day,
And not spending all my time in play.
And still this rule in my mind shall dwell,
Whatever I do, I will do it well."

"Little by little, I'll learn to know
The treasured wisdom of long ago;
And one of these days, perhaps, we'll see
That the world will be the better for me";
And do you not think that this simple plan
Made him a wise and useful man?

1 Which phrase from the first stanza is an example of alliteration?

- Ⓐ *slowly sank*
- Ⓑ *mossy bed*
- Ⓒ *earth away*
- Ⓓ *sipped the dew*

2 Read this line from the poem.

> **"Moment by moment, I'll well employ,**

As it is used in the line, what does "well employ" refer to?

- Ⓐ getting a job
- Ⓑ having a good attitude
- Ⓒ using one's time wisely
- Ⓓ working with other people

3 In the poem, the phrase "little by little" uses repetition. The poet also uses repetition to represent time passing. Complete the table by listing **three** examples of repetition representing time passing.

Examples of Repetition
1)
2)
3)

4 Complete the diagram by adding the **three** other changes that occurred as the acorn became an oak tree.

How the Acorn Became an Oak Tree

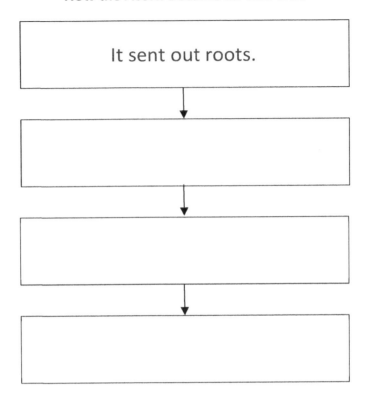

5 Read this line from the poem.

Till the mighty oak is the forest's pride.

What does this line mainly reveal?

- Ⓐ how great the oak became
- Ⓑ how long it took for the oak to grow
- Ⓒ how important the oak is to the forest
- Ⓓ how the oak lived for a long time

6 What does the poet mainly want the reader to know?

- Ⓐ Nobody achieves anything great without a plan.
- Ⓑ Small actions over time can lead to big results.
- Ⓒ There is no guarantee that hard work will pay off.
- Ⓓ There is too much to learn to learn it all at once.

7 The third stanza describes the boy's attitude toward learning. Describe **two** rules the boy uses to guide his actions.

1: _____

_____

2: _____

_____

8 Describe the subject of the first two stanzas and the subject of the last two stanzas. What is similar about the subjects?

_____

_____

_____

_____

9   Does the photograph suggest that the boy feels relaxed or stressed while studying? Explain how this relates to the boy described in the poem.

_____

_____

_____

_____

_____

10 Describe the rhyme pattern of each stanza of the poem.

_____

_____

_____

_____

_____

The Fox and the Stork

Old Mister Fox, who was known to be mean,
Invited Dame Stork in to dinner.
There was nothing but soup that could scarcely be seen.
Soup *never* was served any thinner.
And the worst of it was, as I'm bound to relate,
Mister Fox dished it up on a *flat* china plate.

Dame Stork, as you know, has a very long beak:
Not a crumb or drop could she gather
Had she pecked at the plate every day in the week.
But as for the fox – sly old father:
With his tongue lapping soup at a scandalous rate,
He licked up the last bit and polished the plate.

Pretty soon Mistress Stork spread a feast of her own;
Mister Fox was invited to share it.
He came, and he saw, and he gave a great groan:
The stork had known how to prepare it.
She had meant to get even, and now was *her* turn:
Mister Fox was invited *to eat from an urn.*

The urn's mouth was small, and it had a long neck;
The food in it smelled most delightful.
Dame Stork, with her beak in, proceeded to peck;
But the fox found that fasting is frightful.
Home he sneaked. On his way there he felt his ears burn
When he thought of the stork and her tall, tricky urn.

1 Which line from the first stanza uses exaggeration?

- Ⓐ *Old Mister Fox, who was known to be mean,*
- Ⓑ *Soup never was served any thinner.*
- Ⓒ *And the worst of it was, as I'm bound to relate,*
- Ⓓ *Mister Fox dished it up on a flat china plate.*

2 Circle **two** phrases from the lines below that show that the fox ate greedily.

> With his tongue lapping soup at a scandalous rate,
>
> He licked up the last bit and polished the plate.

3 Select **all** the lines below that contain alliteration.

- ☐ He came, and he saw, and he gave a great groan:
- ☐ The stork had known how to prepare it.
- ☐ The urn's mouth was small, and it had a long neck;
- ☐ The food in it smelled most delightful.
- ☐ Dame Stork, with her beak in, proceeded to peck;
- ☐ But the fox found that fasting is frightful.

4 The last stanza describes how the fox "sneaked" home. This detail suggests that he feels –

- Ⓐ confused
- Ⓑ embarrassed
- Ⓒ hungry
- Ⓓ lost

5 Which of these describes the main lesson the poem teaches?

- Ⓐ The simple things in life are often the best.
- Ⓑ It is important to think of the needs of others.
- Ⓒ Other people will treat you as you treat them.
- Ⓓ Food is most enjoyed when shared with friends.

6 List **two** details that explain why the stork had no chance of getting any soup when the fox served it.

1: _____

2: _____

7 How do the fox's actions lead to the stork choosing to serve her food in an urn? Use **two** details from the poem to support your answer.

8 What do the illustrations help the reader understand about the difference between eating from the plate and the urn for the stork? Explain your answer.

9   What type of poem is "The Fox and the Stork"?

   Ⓐ   an ode, a poem written in praise of something

   Ⓑ   a narrative poem, a poem that tells a story

   Ⓒ   free verse, a poem without a set pattern of rhyme or rhythm

   Ⓓ   a lyric poem, a poem in which someone expresses emotions

10 "The Fox and the Stork" is based on a fable. Describe **two** things the poem has in common with a fable.

   1: _____

   _____

   2: _____

   _____

Practice Set 8

Nature Myths

Set of Two Myths

Instructions

This set has two passages for you to read. Each passage is followed by questions.

Read each question carefully. For each multiple choice question, fill in the circle for the correct answer. For other types of questions, follow the instructions given. Some of the questions require a written answer. Write your answer on the lines provided.

How the Blossoms Came to the Heather

Only a little while after the earth was made, the trees and plants came to live on it. They were happy and contented. The lily was glad because her flowers were white. The rose was glad because her flowers were red. The violet was happy because, however shyly she might hide herself away, someone would come to look for her and praise her fragrance. The daisy was happiest of all because every child in the world loved her.

The trees and plants chose homes for themselves.

The oak said, "I will live in the broad fields and by the roads, and travelers may sit in my shadow."

"I shall be contented on the waters of the pond," said the water-lily.

"And I am contented in the sunny fields," said the daisy.

"My fragrance shall rise from beside some mossy stone," said the violet.

Each plant chose its home where it would be most happy and contented.

There was one little plant, however, that had not said a word and had not chosen a home. This plant was the heather. She had not the sweet fragrance of the violet, and the children did not love her as they did the daisy. The reason was that no blossoms had been given to her, and she was too shy to ask for any.

"I wish there was someone who would be glad to see me," she said. But she was a brave little plant, and she did her best to be contented and to look bright and green.

One day she heard the mountain say, "Dear plants, will you not come to my rocks and cover them with your brightness and beauty? In the winter they are cold, and in the summer they are stung by the sunshine. Will you not come and cover them?"

"I cannot leave the pond," cried the water-lily.

"I cannot leave the moss," said the violet.

"I cannot leave the green fields," said the daisy.

The little heather was really trembling with eagerness. "I would be honored to help the great beautiful mountain," she thought. At last she whispered very softly.

"Please, dear mountain, will you let me come?" she asked. "I have not any blossoms like the others, but I will try to keep the wind and the sun away from you."

"Let you?" cried the mountain. "I shall be contented and happy if a dear little plant like you will only come to me."

The heather soon covered the rocky mountain side with her bright green, and the mountain called proudly to the other plants, "See how beautiful my little heather is!" The others replied, "Yes, she is bright and green, but she has no blossoms."

Then a sweet gentle voice was heard saying, "Blossoms you shall have, little heather. You shall have many and many a flower, because you have loved the lonely mountain, and have done all that you could to please him and make him happy." Even before the sweet voice was still, the little heather was bright with many blossoms, and blossoms she has had from that day to this.

1 Read this sentence from the passage.

> **Only a little while after the earth was made, the trees and plants came to live on it.**

What does this sentence tell the reader?

- Ⓐ   what the message is
- Ⓑ   who the main character is
- Ⓒ   when the events took place
- Ⓓ   why the events are important

2 Complete the table by describing where each tree or plant chose to live.

Plant	Where It Chooses to Live
oak tree	
water-lily	
daisy	
violet	

3 The passage refers to the "sweet fragrance of the violet." Select the **two** words below that mean about the same as *fragrance*.

- ☐ aroma
- ☐ cheer
- ☐ scent
- ☐ beauty
- ☐ kindness
- ☐ sparkle
- ☐ brightness
- ☐ prettiness
- ☐ taste

4 Read this sentence from the passage.

> **"I wish there was someone who would be glad to see me," she said.**

Based on this sentence, what is the heather's main problem?

- Ⓐ She does not feel loved.
- Ⓑ She does not have blossoms.
- Ⓒ She does not know where she belongs.
- Ⓓ She does not speak up for herself.

5 Describe **two** reasons the mountain wants a plant to cover him.

1: _____

_____

2: _____

_____

6 Which sentence best shows that the heather lacks confidence? Select the **one** best answer.

- ☐ The little heather was really trembling with eagerness.
- ☐ "I would be honored to help the great beautiful mountain," she thought.
- ☐ At last she whispered very softly.
- ☐ "Please, dear mountain, will you let me come?" she asked.
- ☐ "I have not any blossoms like the others, but I will try to keep the wind and the sun away from you."

7 What is the main purpose of the story overall?

- Ⓐ to describe how something came to be
- Ⓑ to tell how someone learned a lesson
- Ⓒ to explain the role of something in society
- Ⓓ to teach an important value

8 The first paragraph describes what each plant likes about itself. How is what the violet and daisy like about themselves similar? Use **two** details from the passage to support your answer.

_____

_____

_____

_____

_____

9 Describe **two** ways you can tell that the mountain is thankful to the heather for helping him.

   1: _____

   _____

   2: _____

   _____

10 According to the passage, why is the heather given blossoms? Use **two** details from the passage to support your answer.

   _____

   _____

   _____

   _____

A Fish Story

Perhaps you think that fishes were always fishes, and never lived anywhere except in the water, but if you went to Australia and talked to the people in the sandy desert in the center of the country, you would learn something quite different. They would tell you that long, long ago you would have met fishes on the land, wandering from place to place, and hunting all sorts of animals. And if you consider how fishes are made, you will understand how difficult this must have been and how clever they were to do it. Indeed, so clever were they that they might have been hunting still if a terrible thing had not happened.

One day the whole fish tribe came back very tired from a hunting expedition, and looked about for a nice, cool spot in which to pitch their camp. It was very hot, and they thought that they could not find a more comfortable place than under the branches of a large tree which grew by the bank of a river. So they made their fire to cook some food, right on the edge of a steep bank, which had a deep pool of water lying beneath it at the bottom.

While the food was cooking they all stretched themselves lazily out under the tree, and were just dropping off to sleep when a big black cloud which they had never noticed spread over the sun, and heavy drops of rain began to fall, so that the fire was almost put out, and that, you know, is a very serious thing in savage countries where they have no matches, for it is very hard to light it again. To make matters worse, an icy wind began to blow, and the poor fishes were chilled right through their bodies.

"This will never do," said Thuggai, the oldest of the fish tribe. "We shall die of cold unless we can light the fire again." He bade his sons rub two sticks together in the hope of kindling a flame, but though they rubbed till they were tired, not a spark could they produce.

"Let me try," cried Biernuga, the bony fish, but he had no better luck. No more had Kumbal, the bream, nor any of the rest.

"It is no use," exclaimed Thuggai, at last. "The wood is too wet. We must just sit and wait till the sun comes out again and dries it."

Then a very little fish indeed, not more than four inches long and the youngest of the tribe, bowed himself before Thuggai, saying, "Ask my father, Guddhu the cod, to light the fire. He is skilled in magic more than most fishes."

Thuggai asked him, and Guddhu stripped some pieces of bark off a tree, and placed them on top of the smouldering ashes. Then he knelt by the side of the fire and blew at it for a long while, till slowly the feeble red glow became a little stronger and the edges of the bark showed signs of curling up. When the rest of the tribe saw this they pressed close, keeping their backs towards the piercing wind, but Guddhu told them they must go to the other side, as he wanted the wind to fan his fire. By and by the spark grew into a flame, and a merry crackling was heard.

"More wood," cried Guddhi, and they all ran and gathered wood and heaped it on the flames, which leaped and roared and sputtered.

"We shall soon be warm now," said the people one to another. "Truly Guddhu is great."

They crowded round again, closer and closer. Suddenly, with a shriek, a blast of wind swept down from the hills and blew the fire out towards them. They sprang back hurriedly, quite forgetting where they stood, and all fell down the bank, each tumbling over the other, till they rolled into the pool that lay below. Oh, how cold it was in that dark water on which the sun never shone! Then in an instant they felt warm again, for the fire, driven by the strong wind, had followed them right down to the bottom of the pool, where it burned as brightly as ever. And the fishes gathered round it as they had done on the top of the cliff, and found the flames as hot as before, and that fire never went out, like those upon land, but kept burning forever.

So now you know why, if you dive deep down below the cold surface of the water on a frosty day, you will find it comfortable and pleasant underneath, and be quite sorry that you cannot stay there.

1   Read this sentence from the passage.

> **Perhaps you think that fishes were always fishes, and never lived anywhere except in the water, but if you went to Australia and talked to the people in the sandy desert in the center of the country, you would learn something quite different.**

How does this sentence suggest that people will feel about the story?

- Ⓐ   amused
- Ⓑ   frightened
- Ⓒ   puzzled
- Ⓓ   surprised

2   Which of these elements of the story does the illustration at the beginning mainly help readers understand?

- Ⓐ   point of view
- Ⓑ   plot
- Ⓒ   setting
- Ⓓ   theme

3   In the third paragraph, what is the main problem caused by the rain?

- Ⓐ   It wets the fish.
- Ⓑ   It puts the fire out.
- Ⓒ   It fills the pool of water.
- Ⓓ   It makes the ground slippery.

4 Complete the diagram below by listing the **three** other fish that try to light the fire in order.

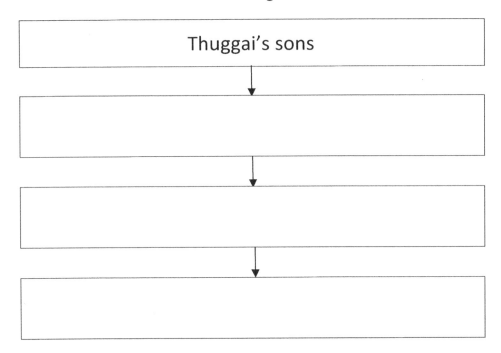

5 Which dialogue shows that they have given up on lighting the fire?

Ⓐ *"This will never do," said Thuggai, the oldest of the fish tribe.*

Ⓑ *"We shall die of cold unless we can light the fire again."*

Ⓒ *"Let me try," cried Biernuga, the bony fish, but he had no better luck.*

Ⓓ *"The wood is too wet. We must just sit and wait till the sun comes out again and dries it."*

6 Circle the **three** words in the sentence below that the author includes to emphasize the power of the wind.

> Suddenly, with a shriek, a blast of wind swept down from the hills and blew the fire out towards them.

7 According to the passage, how is the fire in the water different to the fire on land?

- Ⓐ It feels warm.
- Ⓑ It has flames.
- Ⓒ It does not go out.
- Ⓓ It burns brightly.

8 Read this sentence from the passage.

> **So they made their fire to cook some food, right on the edge of a steep bank, which had a deep pool of water lying beneath it at the bottom.**

Why is the location of the fire important to the events that take place later in the story? Use **two** details from the passage to support your answer.

_____

_____

_____

_____

9 Circle the word that best explains what the fish gain by staying in the water. Then use **two** details from the passage to explain why you chose that word.

      food   shelter   warmth

_____

_____

_____

_____

10 Folktales often start as stories passed on by word of mouth. How does the first paragraph suggest that this is how "A Fish Story" started? Explain your answer.

_____

_____

_____

_____

Practice Set 9

Adventure Story

Khalil's Misadventure

Instructions

This set has one passage for you to read. The passage is followed by questions.

Read each question carefully. For each multiple choice question, fill in the circle for the correct answer. For other types of questions, follow the instructions given. Some of the questions require a written answer. Write your answer on the lines provided.

Khalil's Misadventure

On a foggy day in October, ten year old Khalil found himself lost in the middle of an unfamiliar forest. The day had started out sunny and promising. His dad had taken him and his younger sister, Dalia, down to the lake near their campsite and taught them how to paddleboard. His mom prepared their backpacks with his older brother, Tripp, for their hike later that day. After their morning fun, the family geared up. Khalil and his family had been looking forward to this hike since they arrived at the campsite yesterday morning. This would be Dalia's first time hiking Geronimo Mountain, and Khalil couldn't wait to show off everything he learned from Boy Scouts about navigation and nature.

The family set out to the nearest trail. Geronimo Mountain was one of Khalil's favorite places. He had been going camping with his family since he could barely walk, and he never tired of the views. The hike wasn't too challenging, but it was definitely long. After several miles, the family stopped to enjoy a bagged lunch and rest for a bit.

Without warning, a storm cloud cast a shadow over the family. A crack of thunder made Dalia scream. Then heavy rain came pouring down out of nowhere.

"Quick!" yelled Tripp, "find cover and stay close to the ground!" The family scattered. It was so hard to see that Khalil tripped and started tumbling down the mountain. Khalil's head was spinning so quickly he didn't know which way was up when, at last, he stopped at the trunk of another tree. His legs were badly scratched up and his arms were sore from trying to stop himself. As he slowly sat upright, the rain started to ease up. Confused, Khalil stood and headed in the direction he thought he had come from, only to find an unfamiliar area thick with trees. Khalil had never been on this side of the mountain before.

"Mom!" Khalil yelled. "Dad? Dalia! Tripp!"

No one answered. The clouds remained in the sky, making the forest around him dark and eerie. *What am I going to do?* Khalil thought. Khalil sat and tried to wrap his head around the situation. In that moment, Khalil remembered something he had learned in Boy Scouts: the STOP method. His Scoutmaster had taught his troop that if ever they were ever in trouble, they should use this method which stood for "Stay calm, Think, Observe, and Plan."

Khalil started with step one: stay calm. He took a few deep breaths and brushed the dirt off his knees. Then, he thought. He recalled his family had been traveling uphill and were coming from his campsite located on the north side of the mountain. He looked around him to observe his surroundings. A lone tree in the middle of a small clearing gave him a sign: moss growing on one side. He knew that a tree with access to the sun would grow moss on the north side. Khalil looked towards that direction and saw that it led downhill. That might lead him back to the campsite! Finally, he made a plan. His family would be trying to reunite with him and would likely first return to their tent. There was no way for them to find him here, so Khalil had to follow this downhill direction until he found a footpath. He started walking.

Khalil didn't have any water to keep him hydrated. The thought of this made Khalil even thirstier. With no sign of a river, Khalil remembered another tip he learned in his training: rain water is almost always safe to consume. Thinking quickly, Khalil reached into his pocket to unwrap the poncho he hadn't had time to use when the storm had suddenly hit. Khalil found four twigs and stuck them into the ground. Then he stretched the plastic poncho over each twig until it formed a miniature tent-like structure. He sat back and waited as the rain water fell. After ten minutes, Khalil carefully released the poncho from each twig and tipped the plastic towards him as he gulped down the fresh rain water. He continued on, refreshed.

After about a mile, Khalil spotted a hiker's path! He let out a big sigh of relief. As he jogged downhill on this path, he started to smell the familiar scent of a campfire. Khalil squinted through the branches and made out the yellow tents! He dashed down to the clearing and nearly tumbled over his own feet as he reached his tent.

"Mom! Dad!" Khalil called out. For a moment, Khalil thought he had made a mistake. Maybe his family *had* gone looking for him on the mountain. But then he felt a warm embrace. His mom, dad, brother, and sister wrapped their arms around Khalil and all started talking at once. They were so relieved that they had all found each other again.

That night, as he and his family roasted marshmallows over the campfire, Khalil felt a sense of pride in himself. He had been in a very scary situation but had found his way out using his training and his determination. It had not been the hike he was planning on, but it was certainly a hike he would remember for a very long time.

1. The title of the passage is "Khalil's Misadventure." What does the word *misadventure* tell the reader?

   Ⓐ   The adventure was exciting.

   Ⓑ   The adventure went wrong.

   Ⓒ   The adventure took place outdoors.

   Ⓓ   The adventure never really happened.

2. Use the details in the first sentence to summarize the key features of the story. Write your answers on the lines below.

   Main character   _____

   Setting (place)   _____

   Setting (time)   _____

3. Which sentence from the first paragraph is least important to the main events of the passage?

   Ⓐ   *His dad had taken him and his younger sister, Dalia, down to the lake near their campsite and taught them how to paddleboard.*

   Ⓑ   *His mom prepared their backpacks with his older brother, Tripp, for their hike later that day.*

   Ⓒ   *Khalil and his family had been looking forward to this hike since they arrived at the campsite yesterday morning.*

   Ⓓ   *This would be Dalia's first time hiking Geronimo Mountain, and Khalil couldn't wait to show off everything he learned from Boy Scouts about navigation and nature.*

4   The second paragraph describes how the family stop to eat after several miles. Which aspect of the hike does this detail show?

   Ⓐ   The hike is long.

   Ⓑ   The hike is quite easy.

   Ⓒ   The hike offers great views.

   Ⓓ   The hike is mainly uphill.

5   Read these sentences from the passage.

   > "Quick!" yelled Tripp, "find cover and stay close to the ground!" The family scattered.

   What does the word *scattered* show?

   Ⓐ   Everyone started arguing.

   Ⓑ   Everyone dove to the ground.

   Ⓒ   Everyone shivered from the cold.

   Ⓓ   Everyone ran in different directions.

6   Read these sentences from paragraph 6.

   > No one answered. The clouds remained in the sky, making the forest around him dark and eerie.

   These sentences create a feeling of —

   Ⓐ   calm

   Ⓑ   excitement

   Ⓒ   sadness

   Ⓓ   uneasiness

7 Which step of the STOP method is Khalil doing when he notices the moss growing on the tree?

    Ⓐ   Stay calm

    Ⓑ   Think

    Ⓒ   Observe

    Ⓓ   Plan

8 Complete the diagram below to summarize the steps that Khalil takes to get drinking water.

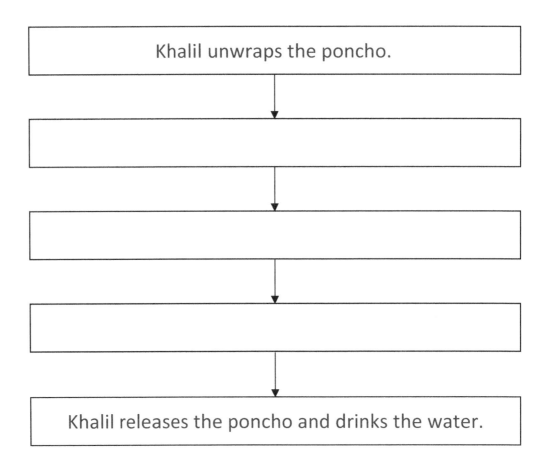

9	Select the **two** phrases from paragraph 9 that show how Khalil was moving.

☐	big sigh of relief

☐	started to smell

☐	familiar scent

☐	squinted through the branches

☐	made out the yellow tents

☐	dashed down to the clearing

☐	nearly tumbled over his own feet

10	What does the family's reaction when Khalil returns to camp suggest?

Ⓐ	They were worried about him.

Ⓑ	They are proud of his actions.

Ⓒ	They knew he would be okay.

Ⓓ	They hadn't noticed he was missing.

11	Paragraph 3 describes the storm. Describe **two** ways the author shows that the storm came suddenly.

1: _____

_____

2: _____

_____

12 How does Khalil get separated from his family? Use **two** details from the passage in your answer.

_____

_____

_____

_____

13 Explain how Khalil's knowledge of nature allows him to determine which way is north. Use **two** details from the passage to support your answer.

_____

_____

_____

_____

14 In the last paragraph, why is Khalil proud of himself? Use **two** details from the passage to support your answer.

_____

_____

_____

_____

15 How does Khalil's experience with the Boy Scouts help him when he gets lost on Geronimo Mountain? Use **three** details from the passage in your answer.

Practice Set 10

Mystery Story

The Creature Caught on Camera

Instructions

This set has one passage for you to read. The passage is followed by questions.

Read each question carefully. For each multiple choice question, fill in the circle for the correct answer. For other types of questions, follow the instructions given. Some of the questions require a written answer. Write your answer on the lines provided.

The Creature Caught on Camera

"Get it away from me!" I yelled from the top of the slide. Arjun knew I was terrified of cats. "Being my best friend doesn't mean you get to torment me."

"Come on, Raylin. She's just a kitten with brown eyes like you," he said, holding the calico up to me.

"I don't care if we both like pizza and dandelions. Lose the hairball," I warned, gripping the pole by the slide entrance. Cats gave me the creeps. The way they stare at you is just terrifying.

"You're no fun sometimes," Arjun muttered, releasing the cat. He saw a crowd of their friends gathering at the other end of the park. "Hey, Raylin. Let's go," he said, pointing to them.

Josh and Alli were my next-door neighbors. They were there holding a tablet and replaying some kind of blurry video. "We can't make it out," Josh said, "but whatever this shadow thing is, it walks like a ghost." It was a grainy, black and white video pointed at their front yard. It crossed at the edge where our yards met.

"I wish Dad didn't pick the cheap motion-activated camera," Alli commented.

"Well, why don't we look at the area this thing was seen at? Maybe there are tracks," I said, pushing my glasses back up to my eyes. Everyone nodded.

Our neighborhood was next to downtown and set up into perfect squares. All the houses were either white or gray except for my house. It was the only one with purple trim, purple shutters, and four plastic flamingos placed in the flower bed in front.

As we arrived at the intersection of our front yards, all we could see was grass. There were no big dirt areas. I did notice something long and off-white wedged in the ground. It was some kind of bone from a small animal. "Maybe it was eating something," I thought aloud.

"There aren't any woods for miles though, and the biggest dog we know is Sam. He's just an old Labrador, and he doesn't move fast like the creature on the video," Arjun commented.

"Yeah, he doesn't really leave his yard either," Josh added.

"Josh, stand right there." I walked backwards towards the mounted camera and replayed the tablet video. "Wow! This creature is almost as tall as Josh." I showed the others what I meant as we stood comparing the video clip to where Josh stood.

"Hopping bananas," Alli squeaked.

I looked around the yard and thought for a moment. "How about we set a trap for it? Maybe we can get a better video shot."

"Good idea," the other kids mentioned.

"Arjun and Josh. Why don't you guys find some meat? Alli, you set the notifications and check the memory for the camera system. The rest of you can help me get something from my backyard."

We all split up into different directions. My group and I dragged a large plastic green turtle. It was the size of my bed and filled with sand. "My baby sister won't need this tonight, but maybe we can get some tracks." I brushed off the dust from my hands as we plopped the turtle down. We used the same corner of the yard since the camera was pointing that way.

With some raw steak left on a plate in the sandpit, the trap was set. That night, however, the camera did not record anything. No notifications. Nothing.

That morning we were so disappointed. "Dumb, cheap camera," Alli said as we met by the sandpit.

"Wait a second," I said as I called everyone over. I noticed the meat wasn't touched, but there was a long and deep indent in the sand. It was as if the creature partially leaned low on a leg to check out the food. There weren't many sand details, but it was definitely as long as my leg.

We resolved to ditch the camera and watch the trap again but with our own eyes. It was nighttime again. Arjun, Josh, Alli and I camped out beside my screened-in front porch. It was just enough distance, and with our binoculars, we would catch a glimpse for sure.

A few hours had passed and the moon was high in the sky. Suddenly there was a noise of something moving. We hugged each other in fright. Then, an orange cat creeped out. I jumped twenty feet in the air. "Guys, I can't stay here now," I muttered. I started to race towards the front door, but Arjun grabbed my shoulder.

"Stop, Raylin! Look!"

Across the street, under a dim street light, we saw it. It looked like a gigantic mutant fox. It was as tall as us and had very long skinny legs. Our eyes widened in horror, and we raced into the house.

We had never seen such an animal. After some research, we discovered that it was called a maned wolf. Apparently, he was going to be a new animal at the zoo in downtown. After calling them, the zoo officials found an opened gate and a hole in the ground under the fence. Thankfully, we found their escape artist. It was a mystery solved for us and a big problem quickly fixed by the zoo.

1 According to the passage, what does Raylin find creepy about cats?

  Ⓐ their sharp claws

  Ⓑ their hissing sounds

  Ⓒ the way they stare

  Ⓓ the way they sneak about

2 Read this sentence from the passage.

> **"We can't make it out," Josh said, "but whatever this shadow thing is, it walks like a ghost."**

What does the phrase "make it out" mean?

  Ⓐ create it

  Ⓑ understand it

  Ⓒ see it clearly

  Ⓓ capture it safely

3 Why can't Raylin and her friends see exactly what the creature is when they first view the video?

  Ⓐ The video is too blurry.

  Ⓑ The video is in black and white.

  Ⓒ The creature moves too quickly.

  Ⓓ The creature hides in the shadows.

4 Read these sentences from the passage.

> "Well, why don't we look at the area this thing was seen at? Maybe there are tracks," I said, pushing my glasses back up to my eyes.

What is Raylin suggesting they do?

- Ⓐ set a trap
- Ⓑ look for clues
- Ⓒ find witnesses
- Ⓓ brainstorm ideas

5 Describe **two** reasons the characters decide it was not the Labrador Sam on the video.

1: _____

_____

2: _____

_____

6 Read these sentences from the passage.

> "Josh, stand right there." I walked backwards towards the mounted camera and replayed the tablet video. "Wow! This creature is almost as tall as Josh."

What is Raylin doing in these sentences?

- Ⓐ seeing how fast the creature moved
- Ⓑ understanding where the creature came from
- Ⓒ comparing the size of the creature to Josh
- Ⓓ checking if Josh might have been the one in the video

7 Read this sentence from the passage.

> **"Hopping bananas," Alli squeaked.**

This sentence shows that Alli feels —

- Ⓐ disgusted
- Ⓑ puzzled
- Ⓒ relieved
- Ⓓ shocked

8 Complete the table below by summarizing what each person or group of people does to set the trap for the creature.

Group	Action
Arjun and Josh	
Alli	
Raylin and friends	

9 In which sentence from paragraph 20 is Raylin making a guess about what happened?

- Ⓐ *"Wait a second," I said as I called everyone over.*
- Ⓑ *I noticed the meat wasn't touched, but there was a long and deep indent in the sand.*
- Ⓒ *It was as if the creature partially leaned low on a leg to check out the food.*
- Ⓓ *There weren't many sand details, but it was definitely as long as my leg.*

10 What is the main difference in the plan the second time they set a trap for the creature?

- Ⓐ They use a different type of food.
- Ⓑ They place the trap in a different location.
- Ⓒ They try to spot the creature during the day.
- Ⓓ They watch with their own eyes instead of using a camera.

11 Which sentence uses exaggeration? Select the **one** correct answer.

- ☐ A few hours had passed and the moon was high in the sky.
- ☐ Suddenly there was a noise of something moving.
- ☐ We hugged each other in fright.
- ☐ Then, an orange cat creeped out.
- ☐ I jumped twenty feet in the air.
- ☐ "Guys, I can't stay here now," I muttered.
- ☐ I started to race towards the front door, but Arjun grabbed my shoulder.

12 The last paragraph describes how the zoo found "an opened gate and a hole in the ground under the fence." What do these details reveal?

- Ⓐ how the creature was able to escape
- Ⓑ how dangerous the creature could have been
- Ⓒ why the creature was looking for food
- Ⓓ why nobody recognized the creature at first

13   What is the purpose of the sandpit? How does Raylin think it may help them solve the mystery? Use **two** details from the passage to support your answer.

14   The passage describes how Raylin wants to "set a trap" for the creature. Are they trying to catch it or just observe it? Use **two** details from the passage to support your answer.

15 After Raylin and her friends see the mystery creature on the video, they create a plan to identify it. Summarize the plan that Raylin and her friends carry out. Use **three** details from the passage in your answer.

Practice Set 11

Legend

The Legend of Cincinnatus

Instructions

This set has one passage for you to read. The passage is followed by questions.

Read each question carefully. For each multiple choice question, fill in the circle for the correct answer. For other types of questions, follow the instructions given. Some of the questions require a written answer. Write your answer on the lines provided.

Cincinnatus was a statesman and leader in the time of the Roman Empire. He was greatly respected and admired and stories of his actions became legend. He became a person whose stories were told to show the most valued qualities of a person. This legend tells of one time when he was called upon by his people.

The Legend of Cincinnatus

There was a man named Cincinnatus who lived on a little farm not far from the city of Rome. He had once been rich, and had held the highest office in the land; but in one way or another he had lost all his wealth. He was now so poor that he had to do all the work on his farm with his own hands. But in those days it was thought to be a noble thing to till the soil.

Cincinnatus was so wise and just that everybody trusted him, and asked his advice; and when any one was in trouble, and did not know what to do, his neighbors would call on him.

"Go and tell Cincinnatus," they would say. "He will help you."

Now there lived among the mountains, not far away, a tribe of fierce, half-wild men, who were at war with the Roman people. They persuaded another tribe of bold warriors to help them, and then marched toward the city, plundering and robbing as they came. They boasted that they would tear down the walls of Rome and burn the houses.

At first the Romans, who were very proud and brave, did not think there was much danger. Every man in Rome was a soldier, and the army which went out to fight the robbers was the finest in the world. No one stayed at home with the women and children and boys but the white-haired "fathers," as they were called, who made the laws for the city, and a small company of men who guarded the walls. Everybody thought that it would be an easy thing to drive the men of the mountains back to the place where they belonged.

But one morning five horsemen came riding down the road from the mountains. They rode with great speed, and both men and horses were covered with dust and blood. The watchman at the gate knew them, and shouted to them as they galloped in. *Why did they ride thus? And what had happened to the Roman army?* They did not answer him, and rushed through the gates. Their eyes were wide with fear as they rode through the streets.

Everybody ran after the horsemen, eager to find out what was the matter. Rome was not a large city at that time; and soon they reached the market place where the white-haired fathers were sitting. Then they leaped from their horses, and told their story.

"Only yesterday," they said, "our army was marching through a narrow valley between two steep mountains. All at once a thousand savage men sprang out from among the rocks before us and above us. They had blocked up the way; and the pass was so narrow that we could not fight. We tried to come back; but they had blocked up the way on this side of us too. The fierce men of the mountains were before us and behind us, and they were throwing rocks down upon us from above. We had been caught in a trap. Then ten of us set spurs to our horses; and five of us forced our way through, but the other five fell before the spears of the mountain men. And now, O Roman fathers! Send help to our army at once, or every man will be slain, and our city will be taken."

"What shall we do?" said the white-haired fathers. "Whom can we send but the guards and the boys? And who is wise enough to lead them, and thus save Rome?"

All shook their heads and were very grave; for it seemed as if there was no hope. Then one said, "Send for Cincinnatus. He will help us."

Cincinnatus was in the field plowing when the men who had been sent to him came in great haste. He stopped and greeted them kindly, and waited for them to speak.

"Put on your cloak, Cincinnatus," they said, "and hear the words of the Roman people."

Then Cincinnatus wondered what they could mean. "Is all well with Rome?" he asked. And he called to his wife to bring him his cloak.

She brought the cloak; and Cincinnatus wiped the dust from his hands and arms, and threw it over his shoulders. Then the men told their errand.

They told him how the army with all the noblest men of Rome had been entrapped in the mountain pass. They told him about the great danger the city was in. Then they said, "The people of Rome make you their ruler and the ruler of their city, to do with everything as you choose; and the fathers bid you come at once and go out against our enemies, the fierce men of the mountains."

So Cincinnatus left his plow standing where it was, and hurried to the city. When he passed through the streets, and gave orders as to what should be done, some of the people were afraid, for they knew that he had all power in Rome to do what he pleased. But he armed the guards and the boys, and went out at their head to fight the fierce mountain men, and free the Roman army from the trap into which it had fallen.

A few days afterward there was great joy in Rome. There was good news from Cincinnatus. The men of the mountains had been beaten with great loss. They had been driven back into their own place.

And now the Roman army, with the boys and the guards, was coming home with banners flying, and shouts of victory; and at their head rode Cincinnatus. He had saved Rome.

Cincinnatus might then have made himself king; for his word was law, and no man dared lift a finger against him. But, before the people could thank him enough for what he had done, he gave back the power to the white-haired Roman fathers, and went again to his little farm and his plow.

He had been the ruler of Rome for sixteen days.

1   Based on the second paragraph, when would people most likely go to Cincinnatus?

   Ⓐ   when feeling lonely

   Ⓑ   when needing money

   Ⓒ   when having a problem

   Ⓓ   when looking for work

2   Select the **two** statements about Cincinnatus that are best supported by paragraphs 2 and 3.

   ☐   He is respected.

   ☐   He keeps to himself.

   ☐   He is a strong leader.

   ☐   His advice is valued.

   ☐   He thinks he knows everything.

   ☐   His losses make people feel sorry for him.

3   Paragraph 4 describes a group of "bold warriors." What does the word *bold* mean?

   Ⓐ   careless

   Ⓑ   clever

   Ⓒ   daring

   Ⓓ   rough

4 Which sentence from paragraph 5 best explains why there is nobody in the city to fight or to lead the fight to save the trapped army?

- Ⓐ *At first the Romans, who were very proud and brave, did not think there was much danger.*
- Ⓑ *Every man in Rome was a soldier, and the army which went out to fight the robbers was the finest in the world.*
- Ⓒ *No one stayed at home with the women and children and boys but the white-haired "fathers," as they were called, who made the laws for the city, and a small company of men who guarded the walls.*
- Ⓓ *Everybody thought that it would be an easy thing to drive the men of the mountains back to the place where they belonged.*

5 Paragraph 6 describes the five horsemen arriving at the city. List **two** details that show that the horsemen are panicked.

1: _____

_____

2: _____

_____

6 The passage describes how Cincinnatus "left his plow standing where it was, and hurried to the city." What does this detail help readers understand?

- Ⓐ how quickly he acted
- Ⓑ how determined he was
- Ⓒ how frightened he felt
- Ⓓ how poor his memory was

7 Read this sentence from the passage.

> **But he armed the guards and the boys, and went out at their head to fight the fierce mountain men, and free the Roman army from the trap into which it had fallen.**

What does the phrase "went out at their head" show about Cincinnatus?

- Ⓐ He led the men.
- Ⓑ He inspired the men.
- Ⓒ He protected the men.
- Ⓓ He hid amongst the men.

8 What does the second last paragraph show about how Cincinnatus responds after saving Rome?

- Ⓐ He enjoys being celebrated.
- Ⓑ He does not abuse his power.
- Ⓒ He wants to inspire new leaders.
- Ⓓ He wishes he had not been called on.

9 Which word best describes the role that Cincinnatus plays in the legend?

- Ⓐ explorer
- Ⓑ hero
- Ⓒ teacher
- Ⓓ villain

10   Does the first paragraph suggest that Cincinnatus should be ashamed of now being poor? Use details from the paragraph to support your answer.

11   The passage describes how the people of Rome did not think they were in much danger from the "half-wild men" at war with them. How does the passage show that this was a mistake? Use **two** details from the passage to support your answer.

12   The five horsemen describe how the Roman army is "caught in a trap." Summarize the trap they are referring to. Use **two** details from the passage to support your answer.

_____

_____

_____

_____

13   Circle the word that describes how the Roman army felt when they returned home after defeating the mountain men. Then list **two** details that support your answer.

humble   joyous   embarrassed

1: _____

2: _____

14   The introduction describes how stories of Cincinnatus were told "to show the most valued qualities of a person." Which of these is a main quality that Cincinnatus represents? Select the **one** best answer.

☐ creativity   ☐ loyalty

☐ intelligence   ☐ patience

☐ kindness   ☐ strength

15 How does the ending of the passage show that Cincinnatus puts the needs of Rome ahead of his own? Use **three** details from the passage to support your answer.

Practice Set 12

Personal Narrative

Kelsey's Random Acts of Kindness Week

Instructions

This set has one passage for you to read. The passage is followed by questions.

Read each question carefully. For each multiple choice question, fill in the circle for the correct answer. For other types of questions, follow the instructions given. Some of the questions require a written answer. Write your answer on the lines provided.

Kelsey's Random Acts of Kindness Week
By Kelsey Yates

As a fifth grader at Goodman Elementary School, I have a lot of responsibilities. I am captain of the science team, a cafeteria helper on Tuesdays, a recess monitor on Fridays, and a mathematics tutor every Friday. On top of that, I have a wonderful group of friends who I love to spend time with and parents who I want to make proud! I feel so lucky that I get to enjoy so many different roles but sometimes it can be exhausting!

Last week, I was feeling overwhelmed with a book report due in my English class and a science competition on the very same day. After lunch, I went to my locker to grab my books and found an envelope with my name on it. I carefully opened the mysterious envelope and was surprised by what I saw. Someone had drawn a picture of me dressed up like a superhero! What a difference that picture made. My stresses seemed to melt away. I suddenly felt like I could achieve anything!

Whoever drew the picture must have known that I was feeling a bit exhausted and wanted to cheer me up. There was no note or signature on the drawing – it was a random act of kindness. It spread a smile across my face and felt like a burst of sunshine! I felt special.

For the rest of the day, I walked around knowing that someone believes in me. Someone cares about me so much that they went out of their way to support me. I put the finishing touches on my book report with pride and entered the science competition with confidence. "Wow", I thought, "If one random act of kindness can make a huge difference in my life, I wonder what one whole week of random acts of kindness could do to the lives of students and teachers at my school." So, I decided to find out.

That evening, I told my mom about everything that had happened that day and my idea to spread random acts of kindness around the school. She loved the idea so much that she decided to help. After some brainstorming, she and I set off to the shops to gather supplies. We bought fuzzy felt to make flowers, colorful construction paper to make cards, and a few extra items that would surely bring happiness to someone's day. I was so excited to start my Random Acts of Kindness Week that I could hardly sleep!

On Monday, I decided to acknowledge my favorite teacher, Miss Burke. I arrived at school extra early so I could place a blue envelope on her desk without her seeing me. When she got to her desk, she looked surprised. She opened the envelope right away and let out a giggle. She took out the bright yellow badge and pinned it on her sweater. "Best Teacher Ever", it read. She proudly wore her badge all day and smiled more than I've ever seen her smile.

On Tuesday, I had my sights set on our school janitor who always wears a Seattle Mariners baseball cap. With the permission and supervision of my school counselor, some friends and I decorated his parking space with Mariners' colored chalk. We drew a big baseball diamond and lots of little baseballs. When he got to school that morning, there was pep in his step. He was chattier with the students and seemed delighted to be at school.

On Wednesday, I kept it simple. During recess, I snuck into the classroom and put a small chocolate on each student's desk – even mine! When the bell rang and everyone shuffled back inside, there was a lot of excitement. The students were asking around to find out where the chocolate came from but I didn't tell.

On Thursday, I brought in the colorful felt flowers that I had been working on so diligently. I put one flower in every teacher's mailbox with a little note that said, "Thank you for being a wonderful teacher!" Later, I saw Mr. Clark wearing his flower in his shirt pocket. Miss Rodriguez displayed her flower in a vase on her desk and Mrs. Adams wore her flower in her hair all day long. Everywhere I looked, I could see the joy that these little flowers brought.

Then, on Friday, I realized I had made a big mistake when I had left my fresh baked cookies on the kitchen counter. I meant to give them to my bus driver, Mrs. Williams, who greets me every morning with a beaming smile. I decided that I wasn't going to let the opportunity to be kind go to waste. I climbed up the stairs to the bus and told Mrs. Williams how much I appreciated her and how happy I am to see her every morning. Mrs. Williams paused. I noticed tears in her eyes and wondered what I had done wrong. Then, she smiled and gave me a great big hug.

During my Random Acts of Kindness Week, I learned two important lessons. One is that it doesn't take much effort to make someone's day really special. The other is that a random act of kindness can be as grand as spending 3 hours making tiny felt flowers or as simple as telling someone that you care about them. Although I made other people feel really good, it also felt really good to give. The week inspired me to start a new club: The Random Acts of Kindness Crew. With just one random act of kindness per week, I believe that we can make our school and our community a cheerful place full of smiles and joy.

1 Read this sentence from the passage.

   I feel so lucky that I get to enjoy so many different roles but sometimes it can be exhausting!

   Which word means about the same as *exhausting*?

   Ⓐ confusing

   Ⓑ exciting

   Ⓒ stressful

   Ⓓ tiring

2 In the first paragraph, Kelsey states that she has a lot of responsibilities. Complete the web below by listing **four** examples she gives of these responsibilities.

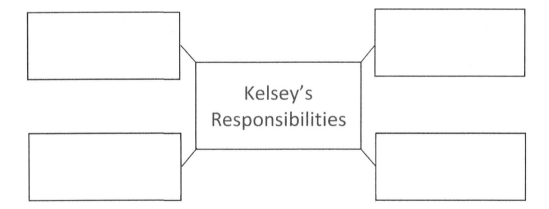

3 Read this sentence from the passage.

> **It spread a smile across my face and felt like a burst of sunshine!**

What does the simile in this sentence emphasize?

- Ⓐ how surprised Kelsey was to receive the drawing
- Ⓑ how puzzled Kelsey was about who left her the drawing
- Ⓒ how great receiving the drawing made Kelsey feel
- Ⓓ how worn out Kelsey had felt before finding the drawing

4 Describe **two** details from paragraph 4 that show how receiving the drawing made Kelsey feel more positive about completing her tasks.

1: _____

_____

2: _____

_____

5 Why does Kelsey decide to do a week of kind acts?

- Ⓐ to help her find out who made the picture
- Ⓑ to make her teachers feel more relaxed and kinder
- Ⓒ to make others feel good like she did
- Ⓓ to show that she can handle more responsibility

6 In paragraph 5, Kelsey describes how she and her mother did "some brainstorming." The word *brainstorming* means that they —

Ⓐ made a budget

Ⓑ thought of ideas

Ⓒ asked others to help

Ⓓ had an argument

7 Which statement best explains why the act of kindness for the school janitor is especially suited to him?

Ⓐ It was based on his love of the Seattle Mariners.

Ⓑ It was carried out with the help of many students.

Ⓒ It was planned for first thing in the morning.

Ⓓ It was done in the carpark instead of in the school.

8 Complete the table below by listing how each teacher displays the flower that Kelsey leaves for them.

Teacher	How the Flower is Displayed
Mr. Clark	
Miss Rodriguez	
Mrs. Adams	

9   Select the **two** sentences that best show that Mrs. Williams was moved by the compliment that Kelsey gave her.

☐   I meant to give them to my bus driver, Mrs. Williams, who greets me every morning with a beaming smile.

☐   I decided that I wasn't going to let the opportunity to be kind go to waste.

☐   I climbed up the stairs to the bus and told Mrs. Williams how much I appreciated her and how happy I am to see her every morning.

☐   Mrs. Williams paused.

☐   I noticed tears in her eyes and wondered what I had done wrong.

☐   Then, she smiled and gave me a great big hug.

10   What does starting the Random Acts of Kindness Crew show about Kelsey?

Ⓐ   She wants to inspire others to do acts of kindness.

Ⓑ   She wants people to know it was her doing the kind acts.

Ⓒ   She doesn't have time to keep doing kind acts all the time.

Ⓓ   She hopes people will do more kind things for her.

11 Look at the photograph of Kelsey at her locker at the beginning of the passage. Do you think the photograph shows Kelsey before or after she finds the picture? Explain your answer.

_____

_____

_____

_____

12 Based on the second paragraph, how did finding the picture make Kelsey feel? Use **two** details from the passage to support your answer.

_____

_____

_____

_____

13   List **two** details that show that Miss Burke appreciated the badge that Kelsey gave her.

   1: _____

   _____

   2: _____

   _____

14   Read this sentence from the passage.

   During recess, I snuck into the classroom and put a small chocolate on each student's desk – even mine!

   Why does Kelsey put a chocolate on her own desk? Explain your answer.

   _____

   _____

   _____

   _____

   _____

15 Write an essay that supports the statement below.

   A simple act of kindness can make a person feel good about themselves.

In your essay, give **three** examples from the passage of an act of kindness that made the person receiving it feel good.

___

Practice Set 13

Play

The Hall of Doors

Instructions

This set has one passage for you to read. The passage is followed by questions.

Read each question carefully. For each multiple choice question, fill in the circle for the correct answer. For other types of questions, follow the instructions given. Some of the questions require a written answer. Write your answer on the lines provided.

The Hall of Doors
Adapted from Lewis Carroll's *Alice in Wonderland*

When the curtain rises one sees nothing but odd black lanterns with orange lights, hanging, presumably, from the sky. The scene lights up slowly revealing Alice *seated on two large cushions. She finds herself in a weird hall with many peculiar doors and knobs too high to reach.*

Alice: Oh! My head! Where am I? Oh dear, Oh dear!

[*She staggers up and to her amazement finds herself smaller than the table.*]

I've never been smaller than any table before! I've always been able to reach the knobs! What a curious feeling. Oh! I'm shrinking.

[*She feels her head and measures herself against the table and doors.*]

Oh! Saved in time! But I never—never—

Humpty Dumpty: Don't stand chattering to yourself like that, but tell me your name and your business.

[*Alice jumps at the voice. Then she looks up and sees Humpty Dumpty sitting on a wall.*]

Alice: My *name* is Alice, but—

Humpty Dumpty: It's a stupid name enough, what does it mean?

Alice: *Must* a name mean something?

Humpty Dumpty: Of course it must; *my* name means the shape I am—and a good, handsome shape it is, too. With a name like yours, you might be any shape, almost.

Alice: You're Humpty Dumpty! Just like an egg.

Humpty Dumpty: It's *very* provoking, to be called an egg—*very*.

Alice: I said you *looked* like an egg, Sir, and some eggs are very pretty, you know.

Humpty Dumpty: Some people have no more sense than a baby.

Alice: Why do you sit here all alone?

Humpty Dumpty: Why, because there's nobody with me. Did you think I didn't know the answer to *that*? Ask another.

Alice: Don't you think you'd be safer down on the ground? That wall's so very narrow.

Humpty Dumpty: What tremendously easy riddles you ask! Of course I don't think so. Take a good look at me! I'm one that has spoken to a king, I am; to show you I'm not proud, you may shake hands with me!

[*He leans forward to offer* Alice *his hand but she is too small to reach it.*]

Alice: What a beautiful belt you've got on. At least, a beautiful scarf, I should have said—no, a belt, I mean—I beg your pardon. If only I knew which was neck and which was waist.

Humpty Dumpty: It is a—*most*—*provoking*—thing, when a person doesn't know a scarf from a belt.

Alice: I know it's very ignorant of me.

Humpty Dumpty: It's a scarf, child, and a beautiful one, as you say. There's glory for you.

Alice: I don't know what you mean by "glory."

Humpty Dumpty: When I use a word, it means just what I choose it to mean—neither more nor less. Now I must be going.

Alice: Goodbye until we meet again.

Humpty Dumpty: I shouldn't know you again, if we *did* meet, you're so exactly like other people.

Alice: The face is what one goes by, generally.

Humpty Dumpty: That's just what I complain of. Your face is the same as everybody has—the two eyes—so—nose in the middle, mouth under. It's always the same. Now if you had the two eyes on the same side of the nose, for instance—or the mouth at the top—that would be *some* help.

Alice: It wouldn't look nice.

Humpty Dumpty: Wait until you've tried it! Good-bye.

[*He disappears as he came.*]

Alice: Oh! I forgot to ask him how to—

[*She tries to open the doors. They are all locked; she begins to weep. She walks weeping to a high glass table and sits down on its lower ledge. She sits on a big golden key and picks it up in surprise. She tries it on all the doors but it does not fit. She weeps and weeps—and Wonderland grows dark to her in her despair. In the darkness she cries, "Oh! I'm slipping! Oh, Oh! It's a lake; Oh! My tears! I'm floating!" A mysterious light shows a "Drink me" sign around a bottle on the top of the table. Alice floats up to it panting, and holding on to the edge of the table takes up the bottle.*]

Alice: It isn't marked poison.

[*She sips at it.*]

This is good! Tastes like cherry tart, custard, pineapple, roast turkey, toffy and hot buttered toast—all together. Oh look, I'm letting out like a telescope.

[*A mysterious light shows her lengthening out.*]

But the lake is rising too. Oh! Oh! It's deep! I'm drowning. Help, help, I'm drowning, I'm drowning in my tears!

Gryphon: Hjckrrh! Hjckrrh!

[*The* Gryphon, *a huge green creature with big glittering wings, appears where* Humpty Dumpty *had been and reaches glittering claws over to grab and save* Alice.]

Reading Skills Workbook, Focus on Fiction, Grade 5

1 Circle **all** the words in the first paragraph below that mean the same as *strange*.

When the curtain rises one sees nothing but odd black lanterns with orange lights, hanging, presumably, from the sky. The scene lights up slowly revealing Alice seated on two large cushions. She finds herself in a weird hall with many peculiar doors and knobs too high to reach.

2 Which of these best describes how Alice seems to feel at the beginning of the play?
- Ⓐ eager and excited
- Ⓑ confused and worried
- Ⓒ curious and fascinated
- Ⓓ lonely and frightened

3 List **two** details from Alice's first lines that inform the reader about her small size.

1: _____

_____

2: _____

_____

4   Read this line from the play.

   Humpty Dumpty: It's a stupid name enough, what does it mean?

   How would Humpty Dumpty most likely sound when speaking?
   - Ⓐ   angry
   - Ⓑ   kind
   - Ⓒ   puzzled
   - Ⓓ   rude

5   How does Alice make Humpty Dumpty feel when she calls him an egg?
   - Ⓐ   amused
   - Ⓑ   curious
   - Ⓒ   insulted
   - Ⓓ   proud

6   Which word best describes the conversation between Humpty Dumpty and Alice overall?
   - Ⓐ   emotional
   - Ⓑ   lighthearted
   - Ⓒ   serious
   - Ⓓ   tense

7 According to the play, why doesn't the key that Alice finds allow her to escape?

- Ⓐ Alice cannot lift the key.
- Ⓑ The key floats away.
- Ⓒ The key does not fit any of the locks.
- Ⓓ Alice is too short to reach the locks.

8 Which sentence spoken by Alice after finding the bottle labelled "drink me" suggests that she is worried about drinking it?

- Ⓐ *It isn't marked poison.*
- Ⓑ *This is good!*
- Ⓒ *Tastes like cherry tart, custard, pineapple, roast turkey, toffy and hot buttered toast—all together.*
- Ⓓ *Oh look, I'm letting out like a telescope.*

9 Which line spoken by Alice shows that she is worried about Humpty Dumpty? Select the **one** best answer.

- ☐ Alice: *Must* a name mean something?
- ☐ Alice: You're Humpty Dumpty! Just like an egg.
- ☐ Alice: I said you *looked* like an egg, Sir, and some eggs are very pretty, you know.
- ☐ Alice: Why do you sit here all alone?
- ☐ Alice: Don't you think you'd be safer down on the ground? That wall's so very narrow.
- ☐ Alice: The face is what one goes by, generally.

10 How do Alice's feelings most likely change when the Gryphon appears?

    Ⓐ   from upset to relieved

    Ⓑ   from angry to calm

    Ⓒ   from excited to scared

    Ⓓ   from confused to alarmed

11 Read these lines from the play.

> **Alice: Why do you sit here all alone?**
>
> **Humpty Dumpty: Why, because there's nobody with me. Did you think I didn't know the answer to *that*? Ask another.**

How do these lines show that Humpty Dumpty is treating Alice's questions like riddles?

_____

_____

_____

_____

_____

12 Why doesn't Alice know if Humpty Dumpty is wearing a belt or a scarf? Explain.

_____

_____

_____

_____

_____

Reading Skills Workbook, Focus on Fiction, Grade 5

13   After Humpty Dumpty disappears, Alice does not finish the sentence below.

Alice: Oh! I forgot to ask him how to—

What did she most likely mean to ask Humpty Dumpty? Use **two** details from the play to support your answer.

_____

_____

_____

_____

14   What problem occurs because Alice is weeping? Use **two** details from the play to support your answer.

_____

_____

_____

_____

15 The play is filled with strange events that could not really happen. Describe **three** strange events that take place in the play. Use details from the play in your answer.

Practice Set 14

Poetry

Set of Two Poems

Instructions

This set has two passages for you to read. Each passage is followed by questions.

Read each question carefully. For each multiple choice question, fill in the circle for the correct answer. For other types of questions, follow the instructions given. Some of the questions require a written answer. Write your answer on the lines provided.

Autumn Leaves
By Angelina Wray

In the hush and the lonely silence
Of the chill October night,
Some wizard has worked his magic
With fairy fingers light.

The leaves of the sturdy oak trees
Are splendid with crimson and red.
And the golden flags of the maple
Are fluttering overhead.

Through the tangle of faded grasses
There are trailing vines ablaze,
And the glory of warmth and color
Gleams through the autumn haze.

Like banners of marching armies
That farther and farther go;
Down the winding roads and valleys
The boughs of the sumacs glow.

So open your eyes, little children,
And open your hearts as well,
Till the charm of the bright October
Shall fold you in its spell.

1 The first stanza mainly makes the scene described seem –

Ⓐ creepy

Ⓑ dreary

Ⓒ exciting

Ⓓ peaceful

2 Select the **two** phrases that best support your answer to Question 1.

☐ In the hush

☐ the lonely silence

☐ chill October night

☐ Some wizard

☐ worked his magic

☐ fairy fingers light

3 The third stanza describes how the warmth and color "gleams through the autumn haze." What does the word *gleams* mean?

Ⓐ fades

Ⓑ falls

Ⓒ shines

Ⓓ sneaks

4 Which of these is the theme of the poem mainly related to?

Ⓐ accepting change

Ⓑ appreciating nature

Ⓒ discovering new things

Ⓓ using your imagination

5 Select the **three** words below that emphasize the brightness of the colors. Tick the box for each word.

☐ sturdy ☐ ablaze

☐ splendid ☐ haze

☐ fluttering ☐ farther

☐ faded ☐ glow

6 Read these lines from the poem.

> **And the golden flags of the maple**
> **Are fluttering overhead.**

What are the "golden flags of the maple"? Explain your answer.

_____

_____

_____

_____

7 In the third stanza, the poet describes the grasses and the vines. How do the words used contrast the color of the grasses with the color of the vines? Use **two** details from the poem to support your answer.

_____

_____

_____

_____

8 Identify the simile used in the fourth stanza. Describe what the simile helps the reader imagine.

_____

_____

_____

_____

9 The last stanza suggests that the season is enchanting and magical. List **two** ways the poet creates this feeling in the last stanza.

1: _____

_____

2: _____

_____

10 The first stanza refers to how a "wizard has worked his magic." Has a wizard really worked magic? Explain your answer.

_____

_____

_____

_____

_____

A Message for the Year
By Elizabeth Clarke Hardy

Not who you are, but what you are,
That's what the world demands to know;
Just what you are, what you can do
To help mankind to live and grow.
Your lineage matters not at all,
Nor counts one whit your gold or gear,
What can you do to show the world
The reason for your being here?

For just what space you occupy
The world requires you pay the rent;
It does not shower its gifts galore,
Its benefits are only lent;
And it has need of workers true,
Willing of hand, alert of brain;
Go forth and prove what you can do,
Nor wait to count o'er loss or gain.

Give of your best to help and cheer,
The more you give the more you grow;
This message evermore rings true,
In time you reap whate'er you sow.
No failure you have need to fear,
Except to fail to do your best—
What have you done, what can you do?
That is the question, that the test.

> EVERY MORNING
> WE ARE BORN AGAIN.
> WHAT WE DO TODAY IS
> WHAT MATTERS MOST.
> — GAUTAMA BUDDHA

1. Read these lines from the poem.

> **Just what you are, what you can do**
> **To help mankind to live and grow.**

What do these lines suggest that people should focus on?

- Ⓐ showing kindness in all situations
- Ⓑ achieving something worthwhile
- Ⓒ being a positive role model
- Ⓓ looking one's best at all times

2. Read this line from the poem.

> **Nor counts one whit your gold or gear,**

What does "nor counts one whit" mean?

- Ⓐ It counts only to yourself.
- Ⓑ It counts more than you expect.
- Ⓒ It does not count anymore.
- Ⓓ It does not count at all.

3. The second stanza refers to workers "alert of brain." This phrase most likely refers to being –

- Ⓐ smart or quick-thinking
- Ⓑ a strong leader
- Ⓒ a good listener
- Ⓓ helpful or supportive

4 Select the **two** lines below that show that you get out of life what you put into it.

☐ Give of your best to help and cheer,

☐ The more you give the more you grow;

☐ This message evermore rings true,

☐ In time you reap whate'er you sow.

☐ No failure you have need to fear,

☐ Except to fail to do your best—

☐ What have you done, what can you do?

☐ That is the question, that the test.

5 Which of these describes the main purpose of the poem?
- Ⓐ to give advice
- Ⓑ to share emotions
- Ⓒ to tell a story
- Ⓓ to describe a scene

6 Which proverb most relates to the theme of the poem?
- Ⓐ All's well that ends well.
- Ⓑ Don't judge a book by its cover.
- Ⓒ Actions speak louder than words.
- Ⓓ Good things come to those who wait.

7 Read these lines from the poem.

> **What can you do to show the world**
> **The reason for your being here?**

How does asking this question engage the reader? Explain your answer.

_____

_____

_____

_____

8 According to the poem, why does nobody have to fear failure? Use details from the poem to support your answer.

_____

_____

_____

_____

9 How does the quote at the end of the passage relate to the poem? In your answer, describe how the poem and the quote have a similar message.

_____

_____

_____

_____

10 Did the poem inspire you? Explain why or why not.

_____

_____

_____

_____

Practice Set 15

Fairy Tale

The Three Tasks

Instructions

This set has one passage for you to read. The passage is followed by questions.

Read each question carefully. For each multiple choice question, fill in the circle for the correct answer. For other types of questions, follow the instructions given. Some of the questions require a written answer. Write your answer on the lines provided.

The Three Tasks
By Jakob and Wilhelm Grimm

There were once two brothers who set out to seek their fortune. They wasted their time and their money in all sorts of foolish ways, and before long they were nearly penniless.
After the two brothers had been gone some time, their younger brother, who had always been thought the simpleton of the family, set out to seek his fortune.

One day as he was passing through a village far away from home, he found his two brothers.

"Where are you going?" they asked.

"I am going to seek my fortune," he replied.

"Ha, ha! How foolish you are!" they cried. "With all our wit and wisdom we have been unable to make our fortune. It is silly of you even to try." And they laughed and made fun of him.

Nevertheless, the three brothers decided to travel on together. As they journeyed on, they saw a large ant hill by the side of the road. The two elder brothers were about to destroy it, when the simpleton said, "Leave the poor ants alone. I will not let you disturb them."

They went on their way until they came to a pond upon which two ducks were swimming. The two older brothers were about to kill them, when the simpleton said, "Leave them alone. I will not let you kill them."

Soon the three came to a tree, in the trunk of which was a wild bee's nest. The two older brothers wished to steal the honey. They started to make a fire under the tree and smoke out the bees. The simpleton said, "Leave the poor bees alone. I will not let you rob them."

At last the three brothers came to a castle where everything looked as if it had been turned to stone. There was not a single human being to be seen. They walked along the great wide hall, but still they saw no one.

"The castle must be enchanted," the brothers said to one another.

After passing through many rooms, they came to a door in which there were three locks. In the middle of the door was a little grating through which they could look into the room beyond.

They saw a little man, dressed in gray, seated at a table. Twice they called to him, but he did not answer. They called a third time. Then he rose, opened the three locks, and came out.

He said not a word, but led them to a table on which a feast was spread. When they had eaten and drunk as much as they wished, the old man showed each of them to a bedroom. There they rested well all night.

The next morning the little gray man came to the eldest brother and beckoned him to follow. He led him to a room in which there was a stone table, and on the table there lay three stone tablets.

On the table near the tablets was written:

"This castle is enchanted. Before the enchantment can be broken, there are three tasks to be performed. The one who performs these three tasks shall marry the youngest and dearest of the three princesses who now lie asleep in the castle. But be warned, there are great punishments for those who fail."

When the eldest brother had read this, the old man gave him the first tablet. On it was written:

"In the forest, hidden beneath the thick moss, are the pearls which belonged to the princesses. They are a thousand in number. These must be collected by sunset. If one single pearl is missing, then he who has sought them shall be turned to stone."

The eldest brother searched the whole day long, but by sunset he had found only a hundred pearls. So he was turned to stone.

The following day the second brother tried his luck, but by sunset he had found but two hundred pearls. So he, too, was turned to stone.

Then it came the simpleton's turn. He searched all day amidst the moss, but he fared little better than his brothers. At last he sat down upon a stone and burst into tears. As he sat there, the king of the ants, whose life he had once saved, came with five thousand ants. Before long the little creatures had found every one of the pearls and piled them up in a heap.

The little gray man then gave the simpleton the second tablet. Upon it was written the second task:

"The key that opens the chamber in which the princesses are sleeping lies in the bottom of the lake. He who has performed the first task must find the key."

When the simpleton came to the lake, the ducks which he had saved were swimming upon it. At once they dived down into the depths below and brought up the key.

The simpleton showed the key to the little gray man, who then gave him the third tablet. On it was written the third task:

"The one who has gathered the pearls and found the key to the chamber may now marry the youngest and dearest princess. He must, however, first tell which is she. The princesses are exactly alike, but there is one difference. Before they went to sleep, the eldest ate sugar, the second ate syrup, and the youngest ate honey."

The simpleton laid down the tablet with a sigh. "How can I find out which princess ate the honey?" he asked himself.

However, he put the key he had found in the lock and opened the door. In the chamber the three princesses were lying. Ah, which was the youngest?

Just then the queen of the bees flew in through the window and tasted the lips of all three. When she came to the lips that had sipped the honey, she remained there. Then the young man knew that this was the youngest and dearest princess.

So the enchantment came to an end. The sleepers awoke, and those who had been turned to stone became alive again. The simpleton married the youngest and dearest princess, and was made king after her father's death. His two brothers, who were now sorry for what they had done, married the other two princesses, and lived happily ever after.

1   Read this sentence from the passage.

   They wasted their time and their money in all sorts of foolish ways, and before long they were nearly penniless.

   What does *penniless* mean?

   Ⓐ   broken

   Ⓑ   lost

   Ⓒ   poor

   Ⓓ   sick

2   Read this sentence spoken by the older brothers.

   "With all our wit and wisdom we have been unable to make our fortune."

   The phrase "wit and wisdom" shows that the brothers think they are –

   Ⓐ   determined

   Ⓑ   funny

   Ⓒ   intelligent

   Ⓓ   lucky

3   Complete the table by listing the remaining **two** animals the brothers meet and what the younger brother stops his older brothers doing.

Animal	What the Youngest Brother Prevents
ants	destroying the nest

4 List **two** reasons the brothers think the castle must be enchanted when they first explore it.

1: _____

_____

2: _____

_____

5 Which line of the instructions near the tablet tell of the reward for completing the tasks?

Ⓐ *This castle is enchanted.*

Ⓑ *Before the enchantment can be broken, there are three tasks to be performed.*

Ⓒ *The one who performs these three tasks shall marry the youngest and dearest of the three princesses who now lie asleep in the castle.*

Ⓓ *But be warned, there are great punishments for those who fail.*

6 According to the passage, what is the punishment for not finding all one thousand of the pearls?

Ⓐ being turned to stone

Ⓑ being changed into an ant

Ⓒ being made to live alone in the forest

Ⓓ being banned from the kingdom forever

7 Why is the younger brother able to collect all the pearls when the older brothers could not?

- Ⓐ He works harder.
- Ⓑ He uses magic.
- Ⓒ He gets help from the ants.
- Ⓓ He is given more time.

8 Read these sentences from the passage.

> **The simpleton laid down the tablet with a sigh. "How can I find out which princess ate the honey?" he asked himself.**

What is the most likely reason the youngest brother sighs?

- Ⓐ He is tired and the tablet is heavy.
- Ⓑ He doubts he can complete the task.
- Ⓒ He is annoyed with being given more to do.
- Ⓓ He thinks that the task will be easy to complete.

9 The story of the younger brother's success mainly suggests the importance of being –

- Ⓐ clever
- Ⓑ honest
- Ⓒ kind
- Ⓓ loyal

10 Paragraphs 6, 7, and 8 describe the three brothers on their travels. How is the younger brother different to his older brothers? Explain your answer.

_____

_____

_____

_____

_____

11 Why do you think the ducks help the younger brother find the key? Use **two** details from the passage to support your answer.

_____

_____

_____

_____

_____

12 How is the bee able to help the younger brother? Use **two** details from the passage to support your answer.

_____

_____

_____

_____

_____

13 List **three** ways the end of the story can be described as a happy ending.

1: _____

2: _____

3: _____

14 How is the use of magic an important part of the plot? Explain your answer.

_____

_____

_____

_____

15 How do the younger brother's actions at the start of the story lead to his success in breaking the enchantment? Use **three** details from the passage to support your answer.

Practice Set 16

Historical Fiction

A Diary of My Time on the Oregon Trail

Instructions

This set has one passage for you to read. The passage is followed by questions.

Read each question carefully. For each multiple choice question, fill in the circle for the correct answer. For other types of questions, follow the instructions given. Some of the questions require a written answer. Write your answer on the lines provided.

A Diary of My Time on the Oregon Trail

From 1836 to 1869, many citizens of the United States were tired of the life on the east coast. Many wanted to find new jobs and buy land to build homes. They did this by starting their journey on the Oregon Trail. This trail was made by fur traders in the early 1800s before many different types of settlers made their way across.

For many, this trip was much more difficult than expected. But, they would not figure that out until they were in the middle of nowhere. They would be out of food, water, and medicine. They would have no way to provide for their families. But, it was the American dream to go west.

Here are a few journal entries of an eleven-year-old settler named Emma. Her family decided to make the journey going west.

April 26, 1837

Dear Diary,

Today we left for California. Papa wants to buy some land and start panning for gold. We got a covered wagon, enough food and water for four months, and four oxen.

In our wagon we will have me, Papa, Mama, my older sister Jane, and my baby brother Henry. We are also traveling with four other families. We should get to California by September.

Papa said he was going to teach me how to fish and hunt on our way to California. But, I am not sure how I will do. I am a good cook, so maybe I can just cook whatever Papa catches. I hope I will make friends with the kids from the other families.

Emma

May 4, 1837

Dear Diary,

Today we stopped at a small town. We were not running low on any supplies. But, it was nice to see other people and get a hot meal that we did not make ourselves. Mama and Jane went to a tailor and each bought a new hat. Papa went to the market to get more dried meats for the road. I was stuck watching baby Henry.

The Smith family has a boy my age named George. He stayed with me so I would not be alone or bored. We played checkers and chess all day. We also talked about our favorite school subjects. Mine is art and his is science.

His parents forgot to leave him something to eat for lunch. So, we shared my dried turkey meat sandwich and apple for lunch. I had a big breakfast in town, so I did not mind sharing.

At dark, Mama, Papa, and Jane came back to the covered wagon. George's parents were running late, so we set up a campfire to wait for them.

Emma

May 17, 1837

Dear Diary,

Breakfast this morning was light. We shared a small pot of oatmeal and each had an orange. By midday, I was already hungry. Every day our meals have been getting lighter and lighter. Papa said he is worried that we did not bring enough food with us. He also heard that water is harder to get as we get closer to California. He said that there are fewer towns on the trail.

Mama is worried because baby Henry is starting to get sick. He has a runny nose and a bad cough. Jane and I must sit with Papa, driving the wagon. She is worried that we will get sick from Henry, too.

I have not seen George in a few days. In the last town we stopped in, they wanted to stay overnight at an inn. On the trail, we sleep on blankets and cots, rather than beds. After a while, your back and neck start to hurt. George's parents wanted to sleep in a real bed for a couple of nights to recover. Hopefully I see George again soon.

Emma

June 1, 1837

Dear Diary,

Baby Henry is finally better. We stopped over for a night in a town that had a doctor. He gave Henry some medicine, and today he is finally better. Jane and I were getting tired of spending so much time in the front of the wagon.

George and his family finally caught back up to us! We had to stop over an extra night to hunt and fish for fresh meat, and they came across us and stopped to hunt and fish as well. George was upset because his dog ran off chasing a rabbit. They waited for half a day, but he did not come back. I feel sad for George.

Emma

July 1, 1837

Dear Diary,

Our trip took a bad turn. We ran out of water and food yesterday. Well, we had to get by on our emergency rations. Jane and I had to share an apple, three pieces of jerky, and one cup of water for the whole day. Jane was nice enough to give me two of the pieces of jerky. She said I was still growing and needed it more.

This morning we got back on the trail with nothing to eat. We stopped at the first town we got to and traded some furs for money. Then Papa used that money to buy food. Thankfully, we had a lot of stuff we could trade for money in order to get more food and water. But, Papa was worried that we could run into the problem of not having enough supplies to trade. So, he said we were going to stay in town for a while.

We were able to get enough money to rent a house to stay in. Papa, Mama, and Jane are going to find jobs to work so that we can save up enough money for the rest of our trip. I hope George is doing well.

Emma

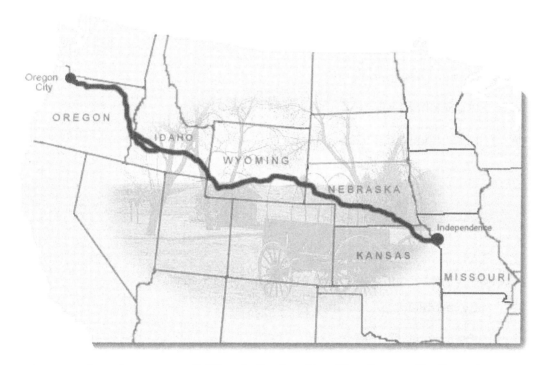

It was a long journey to California for families. The Oregon Trail was just over 2,000 miles long. That would be a long distance to drive today. Can you imagine traveling that far in a covered wagon?

1 According to the passage, who first made the Oregon Trail?

- Ⓐ pilgrims
- Ⓑ fur traders
- Ⓒ early explorers
- Ⓓ cattle farmers

2 According to the first paragraph, why did people decide to make the long journey along the Oregon Trail?

- Ⓐ to have adventures
- Ⓑ to meet new people
- Ⓒ to seek better lives
- Ⓓ to find new land to farm

3 What does the second paragraph mainly summarize?

- Ⓐ the problems people faced
- Ⓑ the dreams people chased
- Ⓒ the challenges people overcame
- Ⓓ the hope that people felt

4   Which **two** features described in the first diary entry are supported by the photograph at the beginning of the passage? Select the **two** correct answers.

- ☐ people traveled in covered wagons
- ☐ people planned to search for gold
- ☐ people were headed for California
- ☐ people took food and water on the journey
- ☐ people passed through beautiful areas
- ☐ people took their whole families
- ☐ people traveled in groups
- ☐ people hunted and fished to find food

5   The passage is set in 1837. What aspect of Emma's trip described in the first diary entry is most likely different than how it would be if the story were set in today's time?

- Ⓐ She is going to learn to fish.
- Ⓑ She wants to make friends.
- Ⓒ She is traveling by wagon.
- Ⓓ She hopes to cook for her family.

6. Complete the table below by listing where each person went and what the person bought when they stopped in the small town on May 4.

Person	Place	Item
Mama		
Papa		

7. Complete the web below by listing **three** problems that are introduced in the diary entry for May 17.

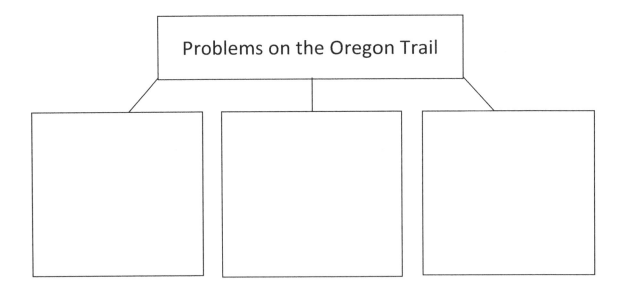

8 In the diary entry for June 1, what **two** positive events make Emma happy? Describe the **two** events below.

1: _____

_____

2: _____

_____

9 Read this sentence from the diary entry for July 1.

> **Our trip took a bad turn.**

What does this sentence mean?

- Ⓐ They got lost.
- Ⓑ The wagon broke down.
- Ⓒ Things went wrong.
- Ⓓ Everyone became sick.

10 On July 1, how does the family get food?

- Ⓐ They get jobs.
- Ⓑ They trade their furs.
- Ⓒ They sell their oxen.
- Ⓓ They ask others to share.

11   In which diary entry do things first start to go wrong? Select the **one** correct answer.

☐   April 26, 1837

☐   May 4, 1837

☐   May 17, 1837

☐   June 1, 1837

☐   July 1, 1837

12   In the diary entry for May 4, how can you tell that Emma and George are becoming friends? Use **two** details from the passage to support your answer.

_____

_____

_____

_____

13   In the last diary entry, why does the family decide to stay in the town? Use **two** details from the passage to support your answer.

14   How does the map and the caption at the end of the passage help readers appreciate the journey that people took? Explain your answer.

15 The second paragraph describes how the trip was much more difficult than many people expected. Explain how Emma's story is an example of this. Use **three** details from the passage in your answer.

Answer Key

Practice Set 1
My Rotten Day at the Beach

Question	Answer
1	B
2	The student should complete the table with the details below. Likes: looking for sea glass, drinking grape soda Dislikes: getting sand in her hair, seagulls squawking
3	A
4	It was as cold as ice.
5	C
6	C
7	B
8	The student should complete the diagram with the events below. Elle steps on a fishing hook. → Elle calls for her father. → Elle's father carries her to the car. → They go to the doctor. → The doctor takes out the hook.
9	A
10	C
11	The student should explain that Elle is disappointed because she does not like the beach that much and thought they might go somewhere better like Six Flags. The answer could also refer to how it was the only day she was not stuck at home.
12	The student should give a reasonable explanation of why the long line would have made the events worse. The answer should refer to how the long wait would make not getting the ice cream even more disappointing.
13	The student should explain that the day does get worse. The answer should describe how she gets a fishing hook stuck in her foot.
14	B
15	The student should give an opinion on what he or she thinks is the worst thing that happened to Elle. The student should include a reasonable explanation to support the opinion and use relevant details from the passage.

Practice Set 2
The Lantern and the Fan

Question	Answer
1	C
2	B
3	A
4	A
5	ambled roamed
6	D
7	B
8	C
9	A
10	C
11	The student should describe the custom that the sons and their wives must always obey the father.
12	The student should describe how all the wise men say that "there is no such paper in Japan." The answer may refer to how the wise men do not think the task is possible or how the wives get the same answer from every wise man they ask.
13	The student should explain that the fan carries wind because when you wave it near your face, the wind is felt on your face, and so the fan must be carrying wind.
14	The student should give a reasonable explanation about how the passage involves a quest. The answer should refer to how the wives are given a task or a mission to return with two items that will be hard to find. The answer should show an understanding that a quest is a journey with a goal and how the goal is often a difficult one to complete.
15	The student should give a reasonable explanation about how the passage shows the importance of loyalty and respect and use relevant supporting details. The answer should refer to how the wives show respect to the father-in-law and prove their loyalty by returning with the gifts he asked for. The answer may refer to how the wives are accepted because they have proved their loyalty and obeyed the father.

Practice Set 3
Christopher Columbus

Question	Answer
1	The student should list how Columbus believed that India could be reached by going west and believed that the world was round.
2	B
3	A
4	B
5	A
6	A
7	The student should complete the web with the three signs below. the birds in the air, the unusual fishes, the plants that are usually seen near rocks
8	C
9	B
10	The student may list how the sailors rush up onto the deck, look out to the west, push and jostle each other, or shout about seeing land.
11	C
12	The student should explain how you can tell that Columbus has done research. The answer may refer to how he says he has proof, how he has a map, or how he says he has been on long voyages and talked to many sailors.
13	The student should explain that Columbus cannot get anyone to support his voyage and almost leaves to try his luck in France. The answer should also explain how a prior believes in him and begs the Queen to help Columbus.
14	The student should describe how Columbus finally gets support from the Queen in Act II and is finally able to attempt his voyage. The answer may refer to how the Queen says that she will raise money for the fleet and fit out an expedition.
15	The student should describe how Columbus had to overcome challenges to achieve success and support the claim with relevant supporting details. The answer may refer to the challenge in getting the funding and support needed to carry out his plan to reach India, the challenge in convincing people that he could reach India by going west, and the challenge of the journey itself.

Practice Set 4
Working on the Railroad

Question	Answer
1	1865 California Central Pacific transcontinental railroad
2	A
3	B
4	The student should list how the men work above a deep canyon and work in intense heat.
5	B
6	D
7	C
8	C
9	A
10	C
11	The student may list how they rest in rickety tents, eat leftover potatoes, heat their food up on a fire, or have sore muscles.
12	A
13	The student should give a reasonable explanation of how the completed railroad would change travel. The student may describe how it would make travel faster, easier, or make it possible for people to travel across the United States. The answer could refer to how the three men dream of traveling across the United States, or how Charlie imagines taking his family across the country.
14	The student should relate Charlie's binoculars to the future he imagines. The answer may refer to how he imagines being able to travel across the country and make friends on the east coast, or how he imagines the railroad finally being completed.
15	The student should give a reasonable explanation of how the situation and shared dreams bring the three men together and use relevant supporting details. The answer may refer to how they are all having the same experience of working on the railroad in difficult conditions, how they chat to pass the time, or how they all dream of a time when the railroad is completed.

Practice Set 5
The Town Mouse and the Country Mouse

Question	Answer
1	The student should complete the web with the items listed below. wheat stalks, roots, acorns, cold water
2	The student may list how the town mouse ate sparingly, only nibbled a little of this and a little of that, or showed that she was only eating to be polite.
3	C
4	B
5	A
6	The student should list how the country mouse dreamed about the city life and how the country mouse gladly said yes when invited to visit.
7	The student may describe the town mouse's food as more delicious, more interesting, higher quality, fancier, or having a wider variety of food. The answer may refer to the specific foods described, to how the food is described as "a very fine banquet," or to how the foods are described as "the most tempting foods that a mouse can imagine."
8	The student should complete the diagram with the three events listed below. A cat mews and scratches at the door. The servants come in to clear the table. The house dogs comes in and sniffs around.
9	The student should explain that the country mouse decides to leave because she would rather have her plain food and simple life and feel safe than feel frightened all the time. The answer should show an understanding that her experience in the city makes her appreciate her country life.
10	B

Practice Set 5
The Rooster and the Fox

Question	Answer
1	B
2	A
3	A
4	The student may list how the fox says "just think of it," how the fox says that he cannot wait to embrace the rooster, how the fox encourages the rooster to come down, or how the fox refers to celebrating the joyful event.
5	B
6	A
7	The student should explain that the fox is trying to get the rooster to come down from the tree. The answer may refer to how the fox asks the rooster to come down so that he can embrace him. The answer may show an understanding that the fox wants to eat the rooster.
8	The student should explain that the rooster does not believe the fox. The answer may refer to how the rooster seems cautious, does not react to the fox's statement by coming down, or ends up tricking the fox by saying that dogs are coming.
9	The student should explain that if the animals had all agreed to be friends, the fox would not need to fear the dogs and so would not run away. The answer should show an understanding of how saying there are dogs coming is how the rooster finds out if the fox is telling the truth.
10	The student should circle the word "clever." The student should describe how you can tell that the rooster is clever. The answer may describe how he does not believe the fox, how he finds a way to check if the fox is telling the truth, or how he outsmarts the fox and makes him run away.

Reading Skills Workbook, Focus on Fiction, Grade 5

Practice Set 6
Mayor Renna's Letter

Question	Answer
1	B
2	The student should list how she is pacing back and forth and how she clenches and unclenches her fists.
3	B
4	D
5	B
6	D
7	D
8	C
9	B
10	The student should underline the three phrases below. a lot could be done, big strides it must take, polish this town into a true gem
11	The student should relate the time to how nervous and panicked Linda feels. The answer should refer to how she only has a short time to finish her acceptance letter.
12	The student should describe how the mindtyper allows Tut to communicate his thoughts to Linda, and how Linda would not know what the dog is thinking without the device.
13	The student should give a reasonable description of how the letter shows that Linda cares about Gemville. The answer could refer to how she believes in the town, wants to make the town better, or wants to be the mayor that the citizens need.
14	B
15	The student should give a reasonable description of how reading Tut's thoughts changes how Linda feels. The answer should use relevant supporting details. The answer should refer to how she feels anxious and unsure of herself before reading Tut's thoughts, and how she feels positive, focused, and confident after reading his thoughts. The answer could also refer to how Tut helps her focus on why she became mayor and what she wants to achieve.

Practice Set 7
Little by Little

Question	Answer
1	A
2	C
3	day after day year after year moment by moment
4	Shoots sprang out. → Leaves appeared. → Branches spread out.
5	A
6	B
7	The student may list how the boy chooses to learn a little each day, chooses not to spend all his time in play, or chooses to do everything well.
8	The student should identify that the subject of the first two stanzas is an acorn or a growing oak tree and that the subject of the last two stanzas is a boy studying. The answer should describe how they are both growing by taking small actions or by improving day by day.
9	The student should identify that the boy seems relaxed. The student should relate this to the boy described in the poem. The answer may refer to how learning a little day by days allows the boy to remain calm or how the boy's attitude helps him stay relaxed.
10	The student should explain that there are three pairs of rhyming lines in each stanza. The answer may state that the first two lines rhyme, the middle two lines rhyme, and the last two lines rhyme.

Practice Set 7
The Fox and the Stork

Question	Answer
1	B
2	The student should circle any two of the phrases below. tongue lapping soup, scandalous rate, licked up the last bit, polished the plate
3	He came, and he saw, and he gave a great groan: Dame Stork, with her beak in, proceeded to peck; But the fox found that fasting is frightful.
4	B
5	C
6	The student may list how the soup is very thin, how the soup was served on a flat plate, or how the stork has a long beak.
7	The student should explain that the stork is getting back at the fox for serving the soup on a plate. The student may refer to how the stork is described as wanting to get even or to how the poem says that "now was *her* turn." The student may also describe how the fox served food in a way that didn't suit the stork, and so the stork does the same to the fox by serving food in an urn.
8	The student should describe how you can tell that the stork would not be able to use its beak to get soup from the flat plate, but can use its long thin beak to reach the food in the urn.
9	B
10	The student may list how the poem features animal characters, describes animals as if they have human qualities, teaches a lesson, or has a moral.

Practice Set 8
How the Blossoms Came to the Heather

Question	Answer
1	C
2	The student should complete the table with the details below. oak tree – in broad fields, by roads water-lily – on ponds daisy – in sunny fields violet – near mossy stones
3	aroma scent
4	A
5	The student should list how the mountain wants to keep warm in winter and to have shade from the hot sun in summer.
6	"I have not any blossoms like the others, but I will try to keep the wind and the sun away from you."
7	A
8	The student should explain that both the violet and the daisy are loved or appreciated. The answer should refer to how people come to look for the violet and praise her and how every child loves the daisy.
9	The student should list how the mountain says he will be "contented and happy" to have the heather and how he calls proudly to the other plants and tells them how beautiful the heather is.
10	The student should explain that the heather was given blossoms because she helped the mountain or because it was a reward for her kindness. The answer should refer to how a voice says that the heather will have many flowers because she loved the mountain and did all that she could to make him happy.

Practice Set 8
A Fish Story

Question	Answer
1	D
2	C
3	B
4	The student should complete the diagram with the three fish below. Biernuga, the bony fish Kumbal, the bream Guddhu, the cod
5	D
6	The student should circle the three words below. shriek, blast, swept
7	C
8	The student should relate the location of the fire to how the fish fall into the water later in the story. The answer may refer to how they jump back and fall down the steep bank and how the fish and the fire fall into the pool of water.
9	The student should circle the word "warmth." The student should give a reasonable explanation to support the choice. The answer may refer to how the fish were trying to stay warm on land, how the fish gathered around the fire, how the fire in the water kept burning and did not go out, or how the water is described as "comfortable and pleasant."
10	The student should give a reasonable description of how the first paragraph suggests that the story started as a story passed on by word of mouth. The answer should refer to how the author mentions talking to the people in the sandy desert of Australia. The answer may describe how the first paragraph suggests that this is the story the people would tell you.

Reading Skills Workbook, Focus on Fiction, Grade 5

Practice Set 9
Khalil's Misadventure

Question	Answer
1	B
2	Main character: Khalil Setting (place): forest Setting (time): October day
3	A
4	A
5	D
6	D
7	C
8	The student should complete the diagram with the details below. Khalil unwraps the poncho. → Khalil sticks four twigs in the ground. → Khalil stretches the poncho over the twigs. → Khalil waits for rain water to fill the poncho. → Khalil releases the poncho and drinks the water.
9	dashed down to the clearing nearly tumbled over his own feet
10	A
11	The student should list how the author says the storm came without warning and how the rain comes pouring down out of nowhere.
12	The student should describe how Khalil trips and tumbles down the mountain during the storm.
13	The student should explain how Khalil sees the moss and knows that moss will grow on the north side of the tree.
14	The student should explain that Khalil is proud of himself for how he handled the scary situation. The answer may refer to how Khalil describes using his skill and determination to find a way out of the situation.
15	The student should explain how Khalil's experience with the Boy Scouts helps him when he gets lost and use relevant supporting details. The answer should refer to how he remembers the STOP method and follows the steps to find his way back to the campsite safely.

Practice Set 10
The Creature Caught on Camera

Question	Answer
1	C
2	C
3	A
4	B
5	The student should list how Sam doesn't move fast enough and how Sam doesn't leave his yard.
6	C
7	D
8	The student should complete the table with the details below. Arjun and Josh – finds the meat Alli – sets up the camera system Raylin and friends – gets the sandpit
9	C
10	D
11	I jumped twenty feet in the air.
12	A
13	The student should explain that the sandpit is being used to get tracks or prints of the creature, which might help them work out what the creature is.
14	The student should explain that Raylin is only planning to observe the creature. The student may refer to how they want to record the creature or watch the creature come to the sandpit to eat the meat.
15	The student should write a summary of the plan that Raylin and her friends use to identify the creature and use relevant supporting details. The answer should refer to how they use meat to attract the creature, how they place the meat in the sandpit so they can get tracks of the creature, and how they set up the camera to watch the creature the first night and then watch for the creature themselves on the second night.

Practice Set 11
The Legend of Cincinnatus

Question	Answer
1	C
2	He is respected. His advice is valued.
3	C
4	C
5	The student may list how they ride with great speed, how they pass through the gate without stopping, or how their eyes were wide with fear.
6	A
7	A
8	B
9	B
10	The student should explain that he does not need to be ashamed because tilling the soil or doing hard work is thought of as a noble thing. The answer may refer to how he lost his wealth and is poor, but is still hard-working and is respected.
11	The answer should describe how the "half-wild men" trapped the men and caused Rome to be at risk of being taken over. The answer may refer to how the returning horsemen fear that "every man will be slain" and "our city will be taken" or to how the fathers feel as if there is no hope. The answer should show an understanding that Rome was at great risk and that the mountain men were underestimated.
12	The student should summarize how the Roman army are trapped in a valley. The answer should refer to how the mountain men block the entry and exit so the army cannot escape, and attack them from above.
13	The student should circle the word "joyous." The student should list how the army comes home with banners flying and with shouts of victory.
14	loyalty
15	The student should give a reasonable explanation of how Cincinnatus puts the needs of Rome ahead of his own and use relevant supporting details. The answer should refer to how he takes on power to save Rome and how he has the power to make himself king and rule the Romans, but gives the power back to the fathers and returns to his home once his task of saving Rome is complete. The answer should show an understanding that he acts for the good of Rome instead of for selfish reasons.

Reading Skills Workbook, Focus on Fiction, Grade 5

Practice Set 12
Kelsey's Random Acts of Kindness Week

Question	Answer
1	D
2	The student should complete the web with the examples below. captain of the science team, cafeteria helper, recess monitor, mathematics tutor
3	C
4	The student should list how Kelsey put the finishing touches on her book report with pride and how she entered the science competition with confidence.
5	C
6	B
7	A
8	The student should complete the table with the details below. Mr. Clark – wears it in his shirt pocket Miss Rodriguez – has it in a vase on her desk Mrs. Adams – wears it in her hair
9	I noticed tears in her eyes and wondered what I had done wrong. Then, she smiled and gave me a great big hug.
10	A
11	The student should infer that the photograph shows Kelsey before she finds the picture. The answer should refer to how she looks tired and stressed in the photograph.
12	The student should describe how finding the picture makes Kelsey feel calm, less stressed, confident, or positive. The answer should refer to how she says that her stresses melted away and that she felt like she could achieve anything.
13	The student may list how Miss Burke giggled, pinned the badge on her sweater right away, proudly wore the badge all day, or smiled all day.
14	The student should explain that Kelsey put a chocolate on her own desk so that people would not realize that it was her giving out the chocolates.
15	The student should write an essay arguing that a simple act of kindness can make a person feel good about themselves and use three relevant examples from the passage as support. The essay may refer to Kelsey receiving the picture, Miss Burke receiving the badge, the teachers receiving the flowers and a note, or Mrs. Williams being praised by Kelsey.

Practice Set 13
The Hall of Doors

Question	Answer
1	The student should circle the words below. odd, weird, peculiar
2	B
3	The student may list how she finds herself smaller than the table, how she says that she cannot reach the knobs, how she says that she's shrinking, or how she measures herself against the tables and doors.
4	D
5	C
6	B
7	C
8	A
9	Alice: Don't you think you'd be safer down on the ground? That wall's so very narrow.
10	A
11	The student should give a reasonable explanation of how Humpty Dumpty's response seems like he is answering a riddle. The answer should refer to how he does not really explain why he is alone, but instead says that he is alone because there's nobody with him. The answer may also refer to how he responds as if Alice was trying to test him or trick him and says "ask another."
12	The student should relate Alice not knowing if Humpty Dumpty is wearing a belt or a scarf to him being shaped like an egg and Alice not knowing if it is around his waist or his neck.
13	The student should infer that Alice meant to ask how to get out of the hall or how to return to her proper size. The answer may refer to how Alice has shrunk or how she is trying to find a way out of the hall.
14	The student should explain that Alice weeps so much that her tears form a lake that fills the room and that she almost drowns in.
15	The student should describe three events from the play that could not really happen. The student may describe Alice shrinking, Humpty Dumpty appearing, Alice having a conversation with Humpty Dumpty, Alice's tears becoming a lake, the potion that Alice drinks and causes her to start growing again, or the Gryphon appearing to save Alice.

Practice Set 14
Autumn Leaves

Question	Answer
1	D
2	In the hush the lonely silence
3	C
4	B
5	splendid ablaze glow
6	The student should explain that the "golden flags" are the maple tree's leaves. The answer may describe how the lines refer to the color of the leaves and to them blowing in the wind.
7	The student should identify that the grasses are described as "faded," while the vines are described as "ablaze." The answer should refer to how the words show that the grasses are dull compared to the bright colorful vines.
8	The student should identify the simile as the description of the sumacs as being "like banners of marching armies." The answer should describe how the simile helps the reader image the long line of trees.
9	The student may list how the poet asks the children to open their hearts, refers to "the charm of the bright October," or tells how the season "shall fold you in its spell."
10	The student should explain that a wizard has not really worked magic. The answer should show an understanding that the changes and sights observed are actually caused by nature. The student may also infer that the poet describes it this way to make the scene seem magical.

Practice Set 14
A Message for the Year

Question	Answer
1	B
2	D
3	A
4	The more you give the more you grow; In time you reap whate'er you sow.
5	A
6	C
7	The student should explain how the question engages the reader. The answer may refer to how the question challenges the reader, encourages the reader to think about his or her purpose, or makes the reader think about how the message relates to him or her.
8	The student should explain that nobody needs to fear failure because it is only important that you do your best. The answer should refer to how the poem says that the only failure to fear is the failure to do your best.
9	The student should relate the message of the quote to the message of the poem. The answer should describe how both are about actions taken, relate to what people choose to do, or suggest that every day is an opportunity to do something important or meaningful.
10	The student should give a personal response stating whether or not the poem was inspiring and include a reasonable explanation of why the student feels that way.

Practice Set 15
The Three Tasks

Question	Answer
1	C
2	C
3	The student should complete the table with the details below. ducks – killing them bees – stealing the honey
4	The student should list how everything looks like it has been turned to stone and how there is not a person to be seen.
5	C
6	A
7	C
8	B
9	C
10	The student may describe how the younger brother is kind or caring and does not want to hurt the animals or how the younger brother wants to protect the animals while his brothers want to hurt them.
11	The student should infer that the ducks help the younger brother because he helped them or because they are grateful to him. The answer should refer to how the younger brother stopped his older brothers from hurting the ducks.
12	The student should describe how the brother needs to work out which princess ate honey and how the bee is able to tell by tasting the honey on the princess's lips.
13	The student may list how the enchantment ends, how everyone sleeping woke up, how those that had been turned to stone became alive again, how the youngest brother marries the princess, or how the older brothers marry the other two princesses.
14	The student should describe how the enchantment and the three tasks that need to be completed to break the spell are the basis of the plot.
15	The student should give a reasonable description of how the younger brother's actions at the start of the story allow him to complete the three tasks and break the enchantment. The answer should use relevant supporting details. The answer should refer to how the ants, the ducks, and the bees that he helped all help him complete one of the three tasks required to break the enchantment.

Practice Set 16
A Diary of My Time on the Oregon Trail

Question	Answer
1	B
2	C
3	A
4	people traveled in covered wagons people traveled in groups
5	C
6	The student should complete the table with the details below. Mama – tailor / hats Papa – market / dried meats
7	The student may list how they are running out of food, how they may run out of water, how the baby is sick, how they do not sleep on beds, or how people get sore backs and necks.
8	The student should list how baby Henry is better and how George catches up with Emma.
9	C
10	B
11	May 17, 1837
12	The student should describe how you can tell that Emma and George are becoming friends. The answer may refer to how they played games, how they chatted about school, or how Emma shared her lunch with George.
13	The student should explain that they stop in the town because they ran out of food and water. The answer should refer to how they are going to get jobs in the town until they have enough money for the rest of the trip.
14	The student should give a reasonable description of how the map and the caption helps readers appreciate the journey that people took. The answer may refer to how you can tell how far people traveled, and how it is amazing that people did this trip in covered wagons.
15	The student should describe how Emma's story is an example of the trip being more difficult than people expected and use relevant supporting details. The answer could refer to how Emma's family ran out of food and water just like the second paragraph describes, and had to stop in a town and get jobs because they did not have the supplies to complete the trip. The answer could also refer to other problems along the way like the baby getting sick.

Made in the USA
Middletown, DE
02 October 2022